Praise for Elaine A. Clark

"Elaine A. Clark, a renowned speech communication coach, author, podcaster, and app creator, sets herself apart from other industry experts by offering a multifaceted approach to elevating individuals' performances across various platforms."

—*International Business Times*

"[*Speak to Achieve*] explores how effective communication extends beyond just voice, incorporating body language, movement, and storytelling to create deeper audience connections . . . Clark introduces physical exercises that help speakers refine their delivery, harness their emotions, and tap into their personal histories. These techniques empower readers to communicate with greater authenticity and impact in any setting."

—*Success Magazine*

"*Speak to Achieve* delves into three critical aspects of effective communication. It encompasses the art of connecting with various audiences, understanding how to apply communication strategies, and incorporating the elements of logic, authority, and emotion into one's speech. The structure exemplifies Clark's balanced application of the rhetorical triangle of ethos, logos, and pathos and her Making It. M.I.N.E.® method."

—*OK!* News

"Elaine emphasizes the significance of emotion, storytelling, content organization, and performance techniques to captivate audiences and guarantee engagement. Her methodology focuses on creating an engaging narrative, structured content, compelling audio format, and an immersive auditory experience."

—*USA Today*

"Elaine A. Clark, a woman of many hats with over 40 years of experience in acting, audio engineering, casting, directing, on-camera work, and voice-overs, offers a multifaceted approach to enhancing individual performances. Her extensive background has earned her helpful insights into emotional intelligence's role in effective communication."

—*LA Weekly*

"Clark emphasizes the importance of body language and spatial awareness. These can influence the perception of confidence and authority in an interview setting. She highlights simple yet effective techniques to 'own' a space during an interview."

—Investing.com

"Elaine A. Clark and her remarkable journey as a trailblazing woman entrepreneur. Besides being an accomplished speech communication coach, Clark is an author, app creator, and podcaster. She has delved into various disciplines, including acting, audio engineering, casting, directing, and voiceovers in her 40-year career. Her extensive experience has shaped her multifaceted approach to improving people's performances across different platforms."

—*CEO Weekly*

"Unknown to many, effective communication is less about delivering a message and more about establishing a connection. Elaine A. Clark, one of the leading experts in voiceover and communication, states that when speakers share not only the polished parts of their experience but also the vulnerabilities, fears, and setbacks, they build a bridge of understanding. This bridge, founded on shared human experiences, allows the audience to relate more personally."

—*New York Weekly*

SPEAK *to* ACHIEVE

HOW TO BUILD CONNECTION, DEEPEN TRUST, CAPTIVATE AUDIENCES, AND ACHIEVE RESULTS

ELAINE A. CLARK

ALLWORTH PRESS
NEW YORK

Allworth Press books may be purchased in bulk at special discounts for sales promotion, corporate gifts, fund-raising, or educational purposes. Special editions can also be created to specifications. For details, contact the Special Sales Department, Allworth Press, 307 West 36th Street, 11th Floor, New York, NY 10018 or info@skyhorsepublishing.com.

29 28 27 26 25   5 4 3 2 1

Published by Allworth Press, an imprint of Skyhorse Publishing, Inc. 307 West 36th Street, 11th Floor, New York, NY 10018. Allworth Press® is a registered trademark of Skyhorse Publishing, Inc.®, a Delaware corporation.

www.allworth.com

Cover design by Mary Belibasakis
Cover image by Getty Images

Interior images and graphics by Troy Ziel

Library of Congress Cataloging-in-Publication Data available on file.

Print ISBN: 978-1-62153-849-3
eBook ISBN: 978-1-62153-850-9

Printed in the United States of America

Dedication

As I reflect on my entrepreneurial career choices to speak, coach, perform, teach, and write, I realize what a profound influence my parents played. My dad with his military West Point officer training had a commanding voice, an ability to speak different languages, and a talent for storytelling. My mother was a librarian who loved words, both written and spoken. I imagine that if playwright Joseph Stein of the 1963 Broadway show *Enter Laughing* had known my mother, he would have been inspired to write a sequel: *Enter Talking.*

When deciding whether to study music or acting in college, my parents guided me down the performance path. It wasn't exactly because they considered me a superb actor, but rather that they were worried that I'd have a permanent circular callus on my lips from playing the trumpet. Still, music and the musicality of spoken words guide my choices in making words memorable and pleasing to the ear.

Poetry played a role in our home. On nights when a crescent moon was visible, my mother quoted her mother and grandmother: "A scarcely perceptible curve of light, yet it makes the whole sky smile."

Mom & Dad . . . you make me smile, too.

To be fair to my whole family, I also dedicate this book to my husband, three daughters, their husbands, and our three granddaughters, plus to my brother (who lived boldly but left us too soon) and my sister and their families. I extend an additional thanks to all the people I've had the pleasure to cross paths and coach. I have learned and been enriched by every one of you. I am truly blessed.

Contents

Foreword ix

Introduction **xi**

PART ONE: CONNECTING WITH YOUR AUDIENCE **1**

Chapter 1: Relationship and Relatability 3
Chapter 2: Structure 12
Chapter 3: Connection 22
Chapter 4: Inspire Action 30
Chapter 5: Create a Bridge 34
Chapter 6: Rhetorical Appeals 39
Chapter 7: Connecting with the Audience: Checklist 43

PART TWO: TECHNIQUES TO ACHIEVE **45**

Chapter 1: Making It M.I.N.E.®: Overview 47
Chapter 2: Making It M.I.N.E.®: Performance Application 55
Chapter 3: Speaker's Power Box 68
Chapter 4: Storytelling 71

PART THREE: OVERCOMING OBSTACLES **73**

Chapter 1: Performance Pitfalls 75
Chapter 2: Change a Negative to a Positive 77
Chapter 3: Movement Adjustments 79
Chapter 4: Procrastination 83
Chapter 5: High-Pitched Voice 86
Chapter 6: Disorganization 89
Chapter 7: Overthinking 91
Chapter 8: Fear of Public Speaking 93
Chapter 9: Uptalk 95
Chapter 10: Fast Talker 97
Chapter 11: Slow Talker 98
Chapter 12: Confidence 100

PART FOUR: ADAPTING TO SPECIFIC AUDIENCES **103**

Chapter 1: Three Ways to Engage the Audience 105
Chapter 2: Interview Tips, Techniques, and Trends 108

Chapter 3: Business 110
Chapter 4: Personal 113
Chapter 5: Podcasting 114
Chapter 6: Presentations 119
Chapter 7: Speeches 126
Chapter 8: Politics 130
Chapter 9: Job Interviews 132
Chapter 10: TV or Social Media Hosting and Guesting 135
Chapter 11: Sales 139
Chapter 12: Legal 141
Chapter 13: Religion 146
Chapter 14: News 150
Chapter 15: Sports 157
Chapter 16: Social Media Influencers 160
Chapter 17: Voice Overs 162
Chapter 18: Gaming 165
Chapter 19: Disabilities and Additional Needs 167

PART FIVE: MOVING FORWARD WITH EXCELLENCE 179
Chapter 1: Personalizing Your Message 181
Chapter 2: Developing Your Style 186
Chapter 3: Storytelling 191
Chapter 4: Dividing the Workload into Three Sections 193
Chapter 5: Emotional Colors of Speech 194
Chapter 6: Truth or "Tell" 196
Chapter 7: Trusting the Techniques 200
Chapter 8: Practice: Body Language 201
Chapter 9: Practice: Gestures and Movements 204
Chapter 10: Practice: Logic, Emotion, and Authority 205
Chapter 11: Practice: Voice and Speech 206
Chapter 12: Practice: Script Techniques 208
Chapter 13: What Kind of Authority Are You? 209
Chapter 14: Score Your Speech Success 211

Epilogue 213
Acknowledgments 217
Glossary 219
Index 221
About the Author 223

Foreword

Wondering why I wrote *Speak to Achieve*? Here's a bit of information about my experience, background, goals, and why I'm motivated to improve your business and interpersonal speech communication.

For over forty years, I've coached individual speakers and groups in all areas of communication: Business, Sales, News, Law, Religion, Gaming, Politics, Podcasting, Teaching, Stage, TV, Tradeshows, Voice-Overs, and Personal Speech Improvement.

After graduating college with a BA in Theatre/Speech Communication and a Secondary Education degree, I moved to the San Francisco/Bay Area to pursue stage acting, day player roles in TV and film, tradeshow presenting, on-camera hosting and character roles in corporate videos, and voice-overs. In 1986 I founded and owned Voice One, believed to be the first voice-over school, and I sold it 32 years later.

Additional business background includes radio sales; media buyer; advertising copywriter; casting director and audio director for video games, anime, animation, e-learning, corporate narration, and commercials; audio engineer; and co-founder of a special-needs drama and improvisation program for schools and camps.

I'm the bestselling author of two groundbreaking training books: *There's Money Where Your Mouth Is: A Complete Insider's Guide to Earning Income and Building a Career in Voice-Overs* and *Voice-Overs for Podcasting: How to Develop a Career and Make a Profit.*

Wanting to offer a personal interactive speaking experience, I created two speech and diction apps: *Activate Your Voice* and *Adding Melody to Your Voice.* Both apps support my books and coaching. For audio and visual learners, I created and host the speech communication micro-learning lesson podcast *Real Talking Tips*, available on YouTube and wherever you listen to podcasts.

Tapping into all those experiences and offerings, I'm excited to bring you *Speak to Achieve: Strengthen Your Communication Skills to Build Connection, Deepen Trust, Captivate Audiences, and Achieve Results.* My goal is to provide tips, tricks, and speech communication guidance as well as targeted coaching in specific business applications and in people's personal lives. The information in these pages is not only for you . . . but for *your* listeners, audiences, and interpersonal connections so they can achieve results through your speaking.

May you always *Speak to Achieve.*

Introduction

There are lots of motivational speaking books on the market. Many provide step-by-step instructions on *what* to do.

- Tell a compelling story.
- State an interesting fact.
- Ask a provocative question.
- Include a relevant quote.
- Make eye contact.
- Use gestures.
- Add movement.
- Encourage participation.
- Incorporate visual aids.

And that's great. From my perspective as an actor and communication coach, a major step is missing! That's how to take that brain-locked logical information, drop it truthfully into the heart and gut, empower the speaker to express the message effectively, and achieve powerful results. That's a tall task.

How does a speaker aspire to achieve their desired and effective end result? One that:

- Acknowledges and overcomes roadblocks.
- Builds trust between themselves and their audience.
- Constructs a genuine bridge of connection.
- Uses their personal journey to empower others.
- Captivates audiences.
- Achieves results.
- Motivates the audience to think, feel, and take action!

We'll explore a proven speaking method that I developed in the 1990s and use to coach people to get out of their heads, access their emotions at appropriate moments, connect with their personal truth, use specific body movements and gestures to support the message, share their unique personality, and grab and sustain listener attention.

Prepare yourself for an interactive experience. By that I mean, you'll be given little assignments to acknowledge, test, and apply techniques. The goal is to become comfortable creating a story arc so that not only you but your audience of one or more reacts, connects emotionally and intellectually with what you have to say, and feels empowered by the spoken message to take action.

LET'S BEGIN WITH YOUR FIRST ASSIGNMENT

Have you ever thought about your own strengths and weaknesses? It's funny, but people around us often know more about us than we know about ourselves. They tell friends and family members about positive and negative observations and experiences with us.

- Do you have great ideas but struggle to follow through on those great ideas so they become a reality?
- Do you feel that when you speak, you present your message clearly? Then, you're surprised when people ask you to repeat what you just said.
- Do you like the sound of your voice or do you want to improve your speaking voice?
- Do you lack the breath support to sustain and deliver your message?

Practice Assignment

Can you define your personal strengths? Are you creative, friendly, honest, humorous, determined, have a positive attitude? What are your perceived weaknesses? Are you disorganized or a procrastinator? Do you lack self-confidence, talk too fast, have a high-pitched voice, have trouble connecting with your emotions, overthink things, or fear public speaking?

List five of your top strengths and weaknesses in your personal life and as a speaker.

My 5 Top Strengths

1. ______________________
2. ______________________
3. ______________________
4. ______________________
5. ______________________

My 5 Weaknesses

1. ______________________
2. ______________________
3. ______________________
4. ______________________
5. ______________________

Holding a mirror or magnifying glass up to yourself is never easy. Yet, it's a good place to start this communication journey. At the end of this book, you may want to review your notes and see if any items on your list have changed. Knowing who you are is empowering. You have the ability to make people feel and take action. You have a choice to offer a suggestion rather than a demand. You can guide the listener into accepting and adopting your message as their own. When done well . . . it's powerful!

WHAT WILL YOU "LEARN"?

When I started teaching at a university, instructors were encouraged to never state what a person will *learn* because that is subjective. Here's why:

- Personal experiences shape how a person understands and integrates information.
- People process information using different cognitive visual, auditory, and kinesthetic methods.

- Information is absorbed and retained based on a person's motivation, interest, and emotional state.
- Cultural background can impact and prioritize how knowledge is perceived and valued.
- Prior knowledge can facilitate or hinder new learning.
- A person's learning environment can affect how well information is received and processed.

Whatever your style of understanding, grasping, comprehending, mastering, absorbing, discovering, studying, gaining insight, internalizing, becoming proficient, or acquiring knowledge . . . these alternative words add variety and specificity to your script interpretation and speeches.

NUANCES OF THE LEARNING PROCESS

This book is not intended to be passive learning. Prepare yourself for a bit of self-awareness and discovery. If done correctly with an open mind and heart, the outcomes can be immediate and impactful.

Speak to Achieve is divided into five parts, with information specifically targeted to a variety of speaking situations and opportunities.

1. **Connecting** with a variety of audiences and situations: business, personal, podcasts, presentations, speeches, politics, religious, interviews, voice-overs, sales, news anchoring, reporting, sports, PA announcing, and teaching.
2. **Overcoming Obstacles** that get in the way of speaking confidently and with authority.
3. **Utilizing Techniques** like the power of my Making It M.I.N.E.® system—Motivation, Intentions, Need, and Emotions.
4. **Adapting to Specific Audiences**, which requires an awareness of how receptive the audience is to the message, status level, knowledge of the topic, number of people you're speaking to, size or location of the room, movement within the space, adaptability, and how to use the microphone to your advantage.
5. **Moving Forward** with these speech, movement, and body language techniques to incorporate your special attributes,

truth, techniques, logic, authority, and emotion into everything you say.

Get ready to read, practice the techniques, and improve your business and personal communication skills!

PART ONE

CONNECTING WITH YOUR AUDIENCE

For better or worse, HOW we speak impacts others. The foundational elements included in *Speak to Achieve* apply to a cross section of business applications, speech genres, and audiences. While I think it's in your best interest to read all the communication styles and sections, I understand that you may prefer to select areas that specifically align with your personal and business needs.

> **"Speech is power: speech is to persuade, to convert, to compel."**
>
> **—Ralph Waldo Emerson**

CHAPTER 1

Relationship and Relatability

How do you build a relationship with an audience of one or more? And how should the audience relate to what you're saying? Both of those are mighty tall tasks. Let's begin with the **who, what, why, when, where,** and **how** of speaking and writing. These six essential elements help create a structured and thorough presentation of information.

WHO: WHO IS SPEAKING OR INVOLVED?

> "The character of the speaker is a cause of persuasion when the speech is so uttered as to make him worthy of belief."
>
> —Aristotle

Who you are establishes your authority. Who your audience is shapes the tone, structure, information, and status level of the message. Style and attitude change between a speaker and listener based on their familiarity with each other and the subject matter.

When deciding on an approach, the relationship with the audience should be defined on a scale of 1 to 10 or marked on a simple graph like the one below from remote and formal to casual and familiar.

You can choose how professional or relaxed you want the delivery style to be based on the following criterion.

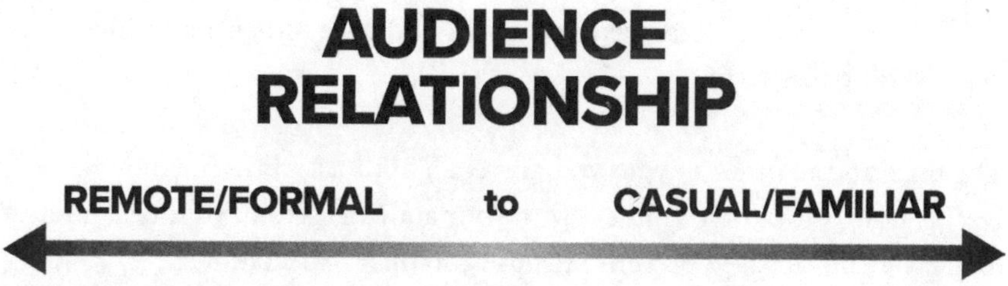

Remote and Formal

1. **Language**: Polished and professional. Slang words and colloquial expressions are avoided.
2. **Tone**: Serious and measured.
3. **Structure**: Formal introductions, summaries, and conclusions are clear, have a logical flow, and include some repetition to reinforce key points.
4. **Engagement**: Interaction with the audience or individual is controlled or somewhat limited. Personal anecdotes and humor are used sparingly. Responses to questions are handled systematically.
5. **Body Language**: Purposeful movements and upright posture.
6. **Delivery**: Deliberate with attention to diction and pacing. Visual aids tend to be more formal and information-heavy.

Casual and Familiar

1. **Language**: Informal. Includes slang, jokes, or idiomatic expressions.
2. **Tone**: Warm, conversational, and relaxed.
3. **Structure**: Looser and more spontaneous. Formalities may be skipped. The speaker might dive right into the main content and allow the conversation to take a natural course.
4. **Engagement**: Interaction with the audience is frequent and more dynamic. Humor and anecdotes are used to keep the audience engaged. To build rapport, the speaker may ask questions and share personal stories.
5. **Body Language**: Casual and relaxed movements and posture.
6. **Delivery**: Natural and expressive. More varied pacing and gestures. Possibly less reliance on formal visuals. The focus is on creating a connection with the audience rather than adhering to a script.

The tone and manner of who you are as an authority is defined by the job. Decide how you want to connect with your audience. It's in your best interest to make a choice based on *your* purpose and *their* expectations.

- Formal settings emphasize professionalism.
- Casual settings prioritize relatability and engagement.

WHAT: WHAT IS HAPPENING OR BEING DISCUSSED?

"For every action, there is an equal and opposite reaction."

—Sir Isaac Newton's Third Law of Motion

Clear communication is an achievable goal. Whether addressing one person or a large audience, it's important that your message be understood the way that you intended. Below is a list of what you should consider, whether writing a script, reading the written message, or speaking extemporaneously.

1. **Purpose**: Know what you want to convey whether it's to inform, persuade, or entertain. Make sure the entire message aligns with your goal. Allow your purpose to guide your content and delivery style choices.
2. **Connection**: Understand your audience's needs, interests, and expectations. Tailor your message to resonate with your audience so that it engages and influences them.
3. **Clarity**: Organize your thoughts logically. Use simple and precise language. Articulate your points clearly so the audience can easily follow, absorb, and retain the information.
4. **Delivery**: What you say is impacted by your tone, pace, body language, and vocal variety. Confidence and expressiveness enhance audience understanding and engagement.
5. **Listening and Feedback**: Effective communication is a two-way street. Be attentive. Acknowledge audience reactions. Adjust your message to meet their needs and ensure that it resonates with them.

What you say needs to be clear and effective, whether it's a casual conversation or in a formal setting. Words have the power to inform, influence, inspire, shape perceptions, and drive actions.

WHY: WHY IS THIS HAPPENING OR IMPORTANT?

"A word after a word after a word is power."

—Margaret Atwood

"Why" is the justification and purpose for speaking. This active intention provides context and relevance for your audience. It's the key motivating factor for people to connect with the message, grasp its significance, and feel motivated to engage with or act upon it.

While there are many reasons someone speaks, below is a list of twenty motivating factors that you should consider using when prepping for or presenting a speech.

1. **Share Knowledge**: Impart valuable information, insights, knowledge, and understanding that can benefit or educate others. Offer personal stories, lessons, and expertise that others can relate to and learn from.
2. **Inspire Action**: Encourage and uplift the audience to take action, pursue their goals, and embrace change.
3. **Raise Awareness**: Highlight and draw attention to important issues, causes, or challenges.
4. **Foster Understanding**: Promote empathy and understanding by bridging anticipated gaps in knowledge and perspective.
5. **Influence Decisions**: Guide audiences to make informed choices or adopt new viewpoints.
6. **Build Credibility**: Establish oneself as an expert or leader in your particular field.
7. **Empower Others**: Provide tools, insights, and encouragement to overcome challenges.
8. **Create Connections**: Build relationships and networks by engaging with like-minded individuals or groups.
9. **Spark Creativity**: Stimulate dialogue to encourage innovative thinking and new ideas.
10. **Lead Change**: Present compelling arguments to drive transformation in a community, organization, or society.
11. **Share Personal Experiences**: Offer lessons learned from personal stories that others can relate to or learn from.

12. **Encourage Growth**: Inspire the audience to grow personally or professionally by embracing new perspectives and challenges.
13. **Entertain**: Provide enjoyment or relief through humor, storytelling, or engaging presentation.
14. **Resolve Conflicts**: Address and mediate disagreements or misunderstandings to achieve resolution.
15. **Advocate for a Cause**: Be the voice for a cause, group, or issue that needs support and attention.
16. **Further Innovation**: Encourage new ways of thinking that can lead to breakthroughs or improvements.
17. **Celebrate Success**: Acknowledge and share achievements by recognizing and motivating others.
18. **Offer Guidance**: Provide direction, advice, or mentorship to those seeking help or insight.
19. **Challenge the Status Quo**: Question established practices and norms by encouraging critical thinking and change.
20. **Leave a Legacy**: Make a lasting impact on others by sharing wisdom, values, and experiences that resonate beyond the current moment.

"Why" fuels passion, guides choices, shapes direction, and transforms ideas into action. It is the catalyst that turns thoughts into deeds, drives purpose and intention, and compels action and decision-making. When you understand the "why" behind any goal, task, or conversation, you are motivated to act with clarity and conviction. Choosing the appropriate reason *why* you're talking snaps the message into shape.

WHEN: WHEN DID IT HAPPEN OR WHEN WILL IT HAPPEN?

> "Have more than thou showest, speak less than thou knowest."
>
> —William Shakespeare's *King Lear*

Knowing "when" something has happened or will happen allows the audience to place the event in a broader timeline, connect it to other events, and grasp its significance.

Five ways a speaker can use "when" include:

1. An exact date, time, or period when the event occurred.
2. A reference or marker that places the event's occurrence in context with the message.
3. A timeline that describes events in sequence or chronological order.
4. A significant milestone that is memorable and links the event to the overall message.
5. A reference to a well-known historical event or time period that relates to and enhances the purpose of the message.

Providing concrete and verifiable details grounds statements in time, enhances credibility, and makes the message more reliable and persuasive. It also helps the audience connect the information to a broader context, reinforcing the speaker's knowledge and strengthening the overall impact.

WHERE: WHERE DID IT HAPPEN OR WHERE WILL IT HAPPEN?

"One place understood helps us understand all places better."

—Eudora Welty

Gesturing to a location, person, or item enhances a speaker's authority and credibility by reinforcing their message with visual cues that demonstrate their knowledge, confidence, and precision. It allows the audience to imaginatively see in their own mind's eye the location the speaker is speaking about. That includes:

- Where something or someone is located in relationship to where they are now.
- The relative size or distance from that location.
- How the speaker feels about that person, place, or thing.
- If the location is stationary (like a building or item on a shelf) or moving (like an airplane or person walking).

Movements, gestures, and personal opinion help enhance the audience's world of imagination.

How does a speaker create this locational 3D world for their audience? Speakers can use the following gestures to convey a specific location.

1. **Pointing**: Directly pointing with a finger, thumb, knuckle, or open hand in a specific direction: in front, behind, on the ground, overhead, or to the right or left.
2. **Sweeping Arm Gesture**: A broad gesture suggesting a general area, region, or range of locations, such as "over there" or "in that direction."
3. **Using Both Hands**: Both hands out and palms facing each other helps describe the relative position of objects or where two places are in relation to each other.
4. **Tapping on a Surface**: Tapping on or touching a map, chart, nearby object, desk, or podium emphasizes a specific location or spot.
5. **Spatial Indication**: Using hand movements to outline a space or shape, like drawing a circle in the air or outlining a square can be used to represent a city, building, or region.

When speaking with the intention of creating a 3D world for the audience, make the gesture and then hold that position. That one- or two-second hold solidifies the stationary position of the "where" location. If the gesture moves, it needs to signify that it is a moving location. For instance, a rocket that shoots up into space or a child that is walking down a hill. Otherwise, a gesture that moves when intended to describe a stationary location can unintentionally imply collapse, flight, or that it's tilting.

When deciding when and where to gesture, keep these points in mind:

- Nouns have locations
- Verbs have actions
- Modifiers encourage awareness and comparisons

I'd be remiss if I didn't warn you that gestures that are *not* organic and spontaneous can appear canned, awkward, and distracting. So, practice in front of a mirror and judge for yourself whether the gestures enhance the message and imagery. If you feel that the gestures are stiff and distracting, shake it off, take a moment to visualize where everything and everyone is located, and try it again. Practice the movement of defining "where" until it feels organic and natural.

HOW: HOW DID IT HAPPEN OR HOW WILL IT HAPPEN?

> "Life is 10 percent what happens to you and 90 percent how you react to it."
>
> —Charles R. Swindoll

The importance of "how" in the "who, what, why, when, and how" framework lies in its ability to explain the process or method behind an action or event. While other elements provide context, purpose, and details, "how" reveals the mechanics, strategies, and steps. Understanding and relating *how* something happens or is achieved adds depth and clarity, making the information actionable and practical. "How" transforms abstract ideas into tangible actions, enabling others to replicate, learn, or appreciate the effort and skill required. In communication, "how" bridges the gap between intention and execution, turning plans into reality.

Here are ten steps to effectively incorporate "how" into speech communication.

1. **Identify the Process**: Understand the steps or methods behind the topic you're discussing. Break down the process into clear, actionable sections.
2. **Ask Yourself "How?"**: Continuously ask "How does this happen?" or "How can this be done?" about your key points. These questions help ensure that you cover the strategy intended or method involved.
3. **Explain Step-by-Step**: Clearly outline the steps or actions involved in your topic. Provide a logical sequence that the audience can easily follow.
4. **Use Examples**: Illustrate the "how" with relatable examples or analogies. This helps the audience grasp complex processes through familiar concepts.

5. **Provide Visuals or Demonstrations**: Where possible, use visuals, diagrams, or demonstrations to show the process and provide a more concrete foundation.
6. **Simplify the Language**: Use straightforward and clear language to explain how something works. Avoid jargon or technical terms that might confuse the audience.
7. **Highlight Key Points**: Emphasize the critical steps or elements in the process. Use phrases like "The key element for doing this well is . . ." or "An important part of this is . . ."
8. **Address Potential Challenges**: Anticipate and explain common obstacles or questions related to the "how." Offer solutions or tips for overcoming them.
9. **Engage the Audience**: Encourage the audience to think about or practice the process themselves. Ask questions like, "How would you approach this?" or "How do you think this works?"
10. **Summarize the "How"**: Conclude with a brief summary of the process. Reinforce the main steps or methods to ensure the audience retains the information.

In addition to the "how" providing practical guidance, it also shapes the emotional tone and attitude of *how* the speaker delivers the message. Audience status level, age range, information knowledge, and receptiveness also shape how the information is presented. Therefore, the same information can be delivered in numerous ways!

One final thought on using the "who, what, why, when, where, and how" framework: Remember that your message should be reciprocal. Don't assume the audience's knowledge and background is the same as yours. While the interest in the topic may be shared, building a relationship and relatability depends on a mutual understanding of the background, information, terminology, outcomes, and expectations. Therefore, consider if it's necessary to simplify or restate complex messages, vocabulary, and acronyms for more inclusive understanding.

CHAPTER 2

Structure

Having spent years in the commercial advertising arena, I've adopted the commercial advertising formula: (1) identify the problem, (2) offer a solution, and (3) empower the audience to take action and make it all seem effortless and easy. How does a speaker do that?

FIVE STRUCTURAL STEPS: THINK, ACKNOWLEDGE, REACT, SPEAK, ENGAGE

> "Before you speak, think; before you react, acknowledge; before you engage, listen."
>
> —Unknown

This quote emphasizes the importance of mindfulness, reflection, and consideration in communication and personal interaction. It starts with an idea that is creative, actively delivered, and has an emotional appeal.

Let's explore how to break down the message, transition the idea into action, and drop the message from the head (idea) to the heart and gut.

THINK

There are two parts to the thinking phase. First is coming up with the idea, writing notes, bullet points, questions, or even the whole script. Second is speaking in the live environment in front of a person or audience where a quick decision is needed to follow through as planned or make adjustments on the fly to the speech, style, or content.

Hopes and expectations are that the thinking, planning, preparing, rehearsing, and speaking go as beautifully as what you imagined in your head. Yet, there's that ornery guy named Murphy with a Law that goes something like this: "Anything that can go wrong will go wrong, and at the worst possible time."

I'll never forget presenting a timed speech to video at a convention. My lavalier microphone slipped off my shirt and fell down my chest. I had to keep going as I tried speaking into the falling microphone while fishing it out from below. The audience was focused and attentive to my plight. After the presentation, the tech audience gave me a standing ovation, and many came up to me to share how they paid more attention to my presentation than anyone else's at the conference. So, be prepared for changes and inconveniences . . . they may be memorable.

There are many reasons why a speaker might need to shift directions and "wing it."

- **Technical Difficulties:** When slides, microphones, or other tech fail, the speaker must adapt by continuing without them, improvising their delivery to maintain engagement.
- **Unforeseen Audience Change:** If the expected audience changes in size, demographics, or expertise, the speaker might need to adjust or adapt their content, tone, or examples.
- **Last-Minute Time Cut:** When the allotted time for the speech is suddenly reduced, the speaker has to quickly decide what key points to focus on and what to eliminate.
- **Repetitive Information:** The host or previous speaker covers some or all of the topics and materials you planned to talk about, forcing you to pivot yours to a new perspective and add information and new topics to fill the time and audience expectation.
- **Host Change of Topic:** If the event host unexpectedly requests a different focus or subject, the speaker must pivot to address the new topic while still remaining relevant.
- **Audience Questions:** A speaker might have to improvise if unexpected or challenging questions arise that weren't anticipated during the preparation and practice.
- **Emotional Audience Reaction:** If the audience reacts strongly—positively or negatively—the speaker may need to adjust their tone, pace, or content to address the mood.

- **Venue or Setting Change:** If a speaker is moved to a different room or location with different acoustics, setup, or size, the speaker might need to alter the delivery style, gestures, and movements to fit the new space.
- **Co-speaker Drops Out:** If a planned co-speaker is suddenly unavailable, the solo-speaker is often expected to cover additional content or shift their approach to fill the gap.
- **New Information or Event:** If breaking news or a significant event occurs immediately before the speech, the speaker should be made aware of it so they can acknowledge and incorporate this newsworthy information into their talk or dramatically pivot the tone or content of the message as deemed necessary.
- **Unexpected Audience Distraction:** If there's an unexpected distraction (like a loud noise or verbal interruption), the speaker may need to pause, acknowledge the situation, and then smoothly continue, or shift their delivery style to regain focus.

In these situations, the ability to stay calm, think on your feet, and adapt to the circumstances is key to successfully navigating the challenges and deliver a compelling speech. This is why many individuals and organizations support and encourage participation in improvisation classes for confidence, flexibility, and team building.

ACKNOWLEDGE

The acknowledgment stage also has two sections. One is right before you speak and the other is sprinkled throughout the message so it feels like a dialogue with the audience rather than a one-sided monologue. Acknowledging the audience or individual helps define how you react, feel, and deliver the message. When walking on stage, this acknowledgment happens as soon as you and the audience see one other.

Step One: "Check in" with yourself immediately before the speaking event. Acknowledge if you're grounded, confident, and ready to go . . . or if you're nervous, apprehensive, or unsure. If you're unready, apply some of the confidence-building techniques described later in this book in Part Three: Overcoming Obstacles.

Step Two: "Read the room" before speaking. Adapt your body language and voice to the environment so you connect with the audience based on their status, expectation, and level of interest. For example, do they need to be relaxed, woken up, taken seriously, or entertained?

Step Three: "Sprinkle in connecting moments" so you continue building the rapport. These could be a reference to a question from the audience, recap of previous information, or a throw forward of what's to come.

The following are ways to acknowledge your audience in each step of this process.

- **Greet the Audience:** Start with a warm, genuine greeting, such as "Good morning, everyone!" or "Thank you all for being here today."
- **Make Eye Contact:** Establish and maintain eye contact with various parts of the audience to convey attention, respect, and engagement. If reading an audio-only script, imagine the person you're talking to is located on the written words and not floating randomly in the air.
- **Use Inclusive Language:** Phrases like "we," "us," "our," and "together" include the audience in the conversation.
- **Refer to the Audience's Role:** Recognize the audience's presence or contribution, such as "As experts in this field . . . " or "I know many of you have experienced . . . " A hand gesture forward is an effective way for a speaker to connect by physically referring to their audience.
- **Tailor the Message:** Show that you understand the audience. Reference their interests, challenges, or your common experiences.
- **Pose Questions:** Ask rhetorical or direct questions that encourage the audience to reflect, mentally and emotionally engage, or directly respond, such as "What about you? Have you ever encountered this situation?"
- **Acknowledge Reactions:** Respond to audience reactions of laughter, applause, or silence, with appropriate comments like "I see that resonates with many of you," "I agree, that's a great point," or "I see you need more information. That's why I'm here."

- **Thank the Audience:** Express appreciation for their time, attention, or participation, either at the beginning or end of the speech.
- **Address Concerns:** Acknowledge any concerns or objections the audience might have. Show that you're aware of their perspective and you're here to help.
- **Encourage Interaction:** Invite the audience to engage, whether through Q&A, a show of hands, or small group discussions.

Taking the time to acknowledge the audience builds rapport, fosters engagement, and improves the chances of your message resonating with those listening.

REACT

There are two crucial areas and purposes for incorporating reaction into speaking. One is physicality to get you out of your head and into your body. The other supports the message content and speaking style.

A physical reaction acts like a springboard to bounce the speaker out of their head and into their body. It should be initiated immediately before speaking and carry through on the first few words. As a result, the logical side of the brain doesn't have time to judge or block the speaker's instincts and plans. Instead, trust takes over.

A genuine and organic movement before speaking adds a spark and sizzle to the opening message. Simple varied physical reactions throughout the message maintains engagement and adaption to the dynamic flow of the presentation.

Here are several ways a speaker can react to an audience, both physically and logically:

1. **Acknowledge Feedback:** If the audience provides verbal feedback or responses, acknowledge it by nodding the head agreeingly and saying, "That's a great point," or gesturing out to the audience while saying "I'm glad you brought that up."
2. **Adapt to Energy Levels:** If the audience seems disengaged or tired, the speaker can increase their energy, use more dynamic gestures, or invite participation to re-energize the room.
3. **Respond to Body Language:** If the audience shows confusion (e.g., frowns, tilted heads, folded arms), the speaker could

mimic their body language, acknowledge that more clarification is needed, and then widen their body language with outstretched arm movements. Or walk to another area to get out of that negative space to regain audience trust and attention.

4. **Incorporate Questions:** If audience members ask questions, the speaker can address them directly during the presentation or confirm that there will be questions at the end.
5. **Adjust Pacing:** If the audience seems overwhelmed or bored, the speaker can change their speed (faster or slower), tempo (adding or removing pauses), or speech musicality (more dynamic or flatter).
6. **Humor and Lightening the Mood:** Everyone likes to laugh. If the audience seems tense or uncomfortable, the speaker can tell a joke or amusing story to lighten the atmosphere and put everyone at ease.
7. **Encourage Interaction:** The speaker can react to a quiet audience by encouraging participation through questions, a show of hands, or small group discussions.
8. **Reinforce Positive Reactions:** If the audience responds well to a point (laugh, nod, applaud, or snap fingers), the speaker can reinforce this by expanding on the point or acknowledging their enthusiasm.
9. **Address Distractions:** If there's a disruption (e.g., noise, technical glitch), the speaker can acknowledge it with a brief comment and smoothly transition back to the topic.
10. **Pivot Based on Reactions:** If the planned content doesn't seem to resonate, the speaker can shift to a more relevant example, story, or angle to better connect with the audience.

Physical and responsive actions and reactions by the speaker demonstrate trust, attentiveness, and adaptability that help establish and maintain a strong connection with the audience.

SPEAK

Speaking styles vary based on the speaker's purpose, audience, and context. As you progress through these five structural steps, you may find that the speaking style you planned is on-target and appropriate or demands a reactionary physical and verbal adjustment.

Here is a list of uses, styles, approaches, and techniques a speaker can choose to convey their message.

1. **Formal:** Used most often in official, professional, or ceremonial settings. It is characterized by structured language, clear articulation, and adherence to protocol.
2. **Informal:** Often used in social gatherings and everyday interactions, an informal style is casual and conversational. The tone is relaxed, with colloquial language, and more personal anecdotes.
3. **Persuasive:** This style often uses rhetorical devices, emotional appeals, and logical arguments. The primary goal is to convince the audience to adopt a specific viewpoint or take a specific action.
4. **Storytelling:** Engaging the audience through a narrative, the speaker weaves a story, using vivid imagery, character development, and emotional arcs to make a point or entertain.
5. **Inspirational/Motivational:** Designed to uplift and energize the audience, the speaker uses powerful language, personal anecdotes, and an enthusiastic tone to inspire change or action.
6. **Didactic/Instructional:** This style is clear and structured, with examples, demonstrations, and step-by-step explanations to teach or explain concepts.
7. **Debate/Argumentative:** This style is logical, assertive, and requires quick thinking and strong evidence. It centers on presenting and defending a position while countering opposing views.
8. **Extemporaneous:** Involves speaking with minimal preparation, often using an outline or key points. The style is natural, adaptable, and allows for spontaneity.
9. **Impromptu:** The speaker relies on quick "on-the-spot" thinking, creativity, and adaptability to address a topic or question.
10. **Conversational:** Relaxed and interactive, the speaker engages the audience as if it's a one-on-one conversation. Dialogue

with the audience is encouraged and often includes questions, comments, or feedback.

11. **Authoritative:** Confident, commanding style based on knowledge or expertise. The tone is assertive with clear and direct language, often used in leadership or crisis situations.
12. **Humorous:** Humor, wit, and anecdotes are used to entertain and connect with the audience. The style is lighthearted and amusing while often delivering a deeper message.
13. **Ceremonial/Epideictic:** Used for special occasions such as weddings, funerals, or award ceremonies, the tone is often respectful, celebratory, or reflective.

As you can see, each speaking style can be effective depending on the purpose, audience, and context. Skilled speakers often blend various style elements together to suit their needs. However, switching extemporaneously from one prepared style to another can be challenging in terms of word usage, body language, and formality.

ENGAGE

Speaking in a manner that engages an audience involves all four of the previously discussed structural steps. Add in some performative techniques and theatrical elements, and your dynamic delivery is sure to captivate, maintain attention, and engage your audience.

Here are some methods to Engage.

1. **Dramatic Pauses:** A strategic—wait for it—pause can build suspense, emphasize key points, develop active listening, and allow the audience to absorb what you've said. Silence, used effectively, is a powerful tool!
2. **Vocal Variety:** Changes in pitch, tone, and volume are dynamic variables to add emphasis and emotion to your speech.
3. **Expressive Body Language:** Movements, gestures, and facial expressions that align with the spoken words reinforce the energy, passion, and meaning of the message.
4. **Movement on Stage:** Unless restricted to one location, don't stay rooted in one spot. Walk around the stage, engage

different sections of the audience, stand still when you're making a point, move when you're formulating a thought or want to get closer to the audience.

5. **Use of Props:** Props used purposefully and in moderation can make abstract ideas more tangible, memorable, and visually reinforce your message.
6. **Storytelling with Characters:** When telling a story, embody different characters with distinct voices, gestures, or stances. This adds depth to the narrative and keeps the audience engaged. Even if you can't change your voice, adapt your body to visually define each character.
7. **Interactive Demonstrations:** Involve the audience in a live demonstration or experiment. This can be anything from a simple hands-on activity to a dramatic reenactment.
8. **Call and Response:** Engage the audience directly with a call and response technique. For example, you ask a question or make a statement, and the audience collectively responds.
9. **Change the Setting:** Enhance the mood or theme by shifting the environment, altering lighting, adding music and sound effects, or rearranging the stage to match different parts of your speech.
10. **Improvise:** Be adaptable and keep the interaction lively by responding spontaneously to audience reactions, unexpected events, or questions.
11. **Rhythmic Speaking:** Use rhythm, repetition, or even a chant-like delivery to make key points more memorable. This can create a sense of momentum and engagement.
12. **Costume or Attire:** Wearing a particular costume or distinctive outfit that relates to the message can make your presentation more visually impactful and thematic.
13. **Engage Multiple Senses:** Combine visuals, sounds, and tactile elements to create a multi-sensory experience. For example, playing relevant music, showing compelling visuals, or even using scents can deepen engagement.
14. **Physical Interaction:** Physical proximity breaks the barrier between speaker and audience. If the setting allows, move into

the audience, shake hands, or pass out objects related to your topic.

15. **Surprise Element:** Introduce an unexpected twist, surprise guest, or reveal a hidden object during your presentation. Surprises can jolt the audience's attention.

These performative techniques transform a speech into an experience, making it more engaging, memorable, and impactful for the audience. Incorporating elements from each of the five structural steps will give your speech "bones" and leave a lasting impression.

CHAPTER 3

Connection

Is it important to connect on a personal level? Do listeners really care about the speaker's background? In most cases, not that much. Unless there's value in your message and how it relates to that individual or group.

CONNECT WITH YOUR AUDIENCE ON A PERSONAL LEVEL

> "People don't care how much you know until they know how much you care."
>
> —Margaret Tyson

Whether giving a speech, presentation, podcast, news report, guest interview, or voice-over recording . . . your connection with the audience is influenced by your status level, a relatable experience, personal history, backstory, and prior moment.

STATUS

High, medium, or low . . . What status are you? The funny thing is that many people don't even know their status level. Some high-status authorities toss off information as if everyone has the same experience and background. That concept hit home some years ago when my piano tuner and musician friend, Steve Benjamins, returned home after months on the road from one of many high-profile singer tours. While adjusting the tension of the piano strings, he casually described an experience "like writing a symphony in your head."

I quickly realized that I had never written a symphony in my head, probably never would, and that he had! In that instant, we shifted from medium-level status friends to symphonically low-status-me and high-status-him.

Acknowledging your status in a given situation establishes that authority doesn't have to be overbearing and powerful but can be casual and relational. A speaker's status level builds trust and credibility. Relative social or hierarchical positions individuals hold within a one-on-one relationship, group, organization, or society are commonly broken down as follows.

- **High Status**—Individuals who hold positions of authority, influence, or experience. They are typically seen as leaders or decision-makers and command respect due to their experience, achievements, or role. Examples: CEOs, experts in their field, senior executives, or respected community leaders.
- **Medium Status**—People that occupy roles that provide some level of influence or authority but are not at the top of the established or perceived hierarchy. They may act as intermediaries, bridging communication between high and low status. Examples: managers, team leads, skilled professionals, or senior staff members.
- **Low Status**—These folks often have limited authority, influence, or experience within the group or organization. They may be new members, junior staff, or those with less power or visibility. Examples: entry-level employees, interns, or new members of a group.

Status levels influence how individuals communicate, make decisions, and interact within different contexts. Understanding these dynamics is essential for effective communication, especially in hierarchical settings. In his comic strip *Dilbert*, Scott Adams shared many examples of Dilbert being awarded or recognized at work only to have that success deflated soon after by a trivial or humbling moment. Status levels change throughout the day based on the situation and the people involved. Maybe that's why women are not fond of the high-status condescension of "mansplaining." (Just sayin'.)

These three status performance tips are quick and effective body movements that I incorporate when coaching speakers. The voice responds to the physical hand placements as up, out, and down movements alter the pitch, sound, and approachability of the speaker.

1. **High**: Hand placement is in the chest area with downward movements. The voice drops lower on the downward gestures to punctuate concepts, ideas, and actions.
2. **Medium**: Hands are waist level with gestures going out. The voice stays in the mid-voice area as hand movements are forward and back to connect on a helpful and unified level.
3. **Low**: Hands below the waist with upward hand movements. The voice starts lower and raises higher when the hands lift up in a casual, down-to-earth manner.

Practice Assignment

Take a moment now to stand up and practice these positions and movements. Read the written descriptions aloud as you place your hands in each described position and gesture with the corresponding down, out, or up hand movement.

PERSONAL HISTORY

Your personal history humanizes you and helps the audience see you as one of them. When a speaker shares aspects of their background, such as challenges they've faced, lessons they've learned, or pivotal moments in their life, it allows the audience to see them as more than an authority figure. They become someone they can connect with who has walked a similar path.

- **Shared Experiences**—By discussing relatable experiences like overcoming obstacles, dealing with failure, or striving for success, the speaker bridges the gap between themself and the audience.
- **Vulnerability**—When a speaker is open about their struggles, mistakes, or fears, it shows humility and authenticity. This vulnerability makes the speaker more approachable.
- **Common Values**—Sharing personal stories that highlight shared values or beliefs (like hard work, perseverance, or

compassion) reinforces a sense of community and mutual understanding.

- **Breaking Down Barriers**—Personal history can dissolve the perceived barriers of status, expertise, or authority, making the speaker appear more like a peer than an untouchable figure.
- **Building Trust**—Audiences are more likely to trust and connect with a speaker who seems genuine. Personal stories that align with the audience's own experiences create a bond of trust, making the speaker's message more convincing.

Personal history helps the audience see the speaker as a real person with whom they can identify, making the speaker's message more persuasive and the connection more profound. How much speakers lean into one or more of these approaches depends on their stylistic approach and the amount of vulnerability they wish to open up and share.

RELATABLE EXPERIENCE

Sharing one or more relatable experiences fosters empathy, making the speaker's message more persuasive and impactful. It's another way a speaker can create a connection with the audience by making the content more engaging, understandable, and memorable.

Relatable experiences serve several key functions:

1. **Builds Rapport:** Sharing experiences that the audience can identify with establishes a sense of camaraderie and trust. The audience feels that the speaker understands their world, which makes them more receptive to the message.
2. **Enhances Engagement:** When a speaker discusses situations or emotions that the audience has experienced, it grabs their attention and keeps the audience interested and involved.
3. **Simplifies Complex Ideas:** Relatable experiences can serve as analogies or examples that make abstract or complex concepts easier to understand. By linking new information to familiar experiences, the speaker helps the audience grasp the message more quickly.

4. **Creates Emotional Resonance:** Personal or shared experiences often evoke emotions. By tapping into these emotions, the speaker can make their message more impactful, ensuring that it resonates on a deeper level.
5. **Increases Memorability:** People are more likely to remember a message that is tied to an experience that they can relate to. By embedding key points within relatable stories, the speaker ensures that the message sticks with the audience for a longer period of time.

Relatable experiences help the speaker bridge the gap between themselves and the audience, fostering a connection that enhances the relationship, engagement, and impact. When you listen to different speakers, especially politicians, it becomes clear how relatable experiences resonate with one audience while they don't resonate and possibly even anger another.

BACKSTORY

Revealing a backstory transforms your message from merely words into a shared experience. It turns the message from a transmission of information into a narrative that the audience can connect with on a personal and emotional level.

Here's why a backstory plays a transformative emotional and actionable role:

1. **Adds Context and Meaning:** A backstory provides the "why" behind the message, helping the audience understand the motivations, challenges, and lessons that shaped the speaker's perspective. This context gives the message greater significance and relevance.
2. **Creates an Emotional Connection:** When a speaker shares their backstory, it often involves personal struggles, triumphs, or pivotal moments. These elements evoke emotions in the audience, making the message more relatable and impactful. The audience becomes emotionally invested in the speaker's journey, which deepens their connection to the message.

3. **Enhances Credibility and Authenticity:** A backstory that includes real-life experiences shows that the speaker's insights are grounded in lived experiences, making the message more trustworthy and authentic.
4. **Humanizes the Speaker:** Sharing a backstory allows the audience to see the speaker as a real person. Relatable experiences add humanity, breaks down barriers, and fosters a sense of shared experience.
5. **Engages and Captivates:** A compelling backstory can capture the audience's attention. By weaving the message into a narrative, the speaker creates a journey that the audience is eager to follow.
6. **Illustrates Key Points:** The backstory can serve as a powerful illustration of the key points the speaker wants to convey. By tying lessons or messages to specific moments in their life, the speaker makes abstract concepts more concrete and relatable.
7. **Encourages Reflection and Action:** A backstory often encourages the audience to reflect on their own experiences in light of the speaker's journey. This reflection can inspire action, as the audience may see parallels in their own lives and feel motivated to make changes or take steps based on the speaker's message.

Actors create backstories for their characters so they know how to feel and react to people and situations. A speaker's personal backstory transforms the message, too, by adding emotional depth, context, and relatability, turning the communication into a shared experience that resonates deeply with the audience. Sharing this experience and transformation makes the message more impactful, memorable, and inspiring.

PRIOR MOMENT

A "prior moment" refers to a significant event, experience, or point in time that occurred before the current context of the speech or presentation. It should spark action and an emotional shift as the speaker moves from the past to the current moment. Effectively delivered, that past-to-present story arc movement should resonate with your audience so it's more compelling, authentic, relatable, and persuasive.

Incorporating a prior moment can make a speech more compelling in the following ways:

1. **Provides Context:** A prior moment offers the audience important background information that helps them understand the relevance and significance of the current message. It sets the stage for what's being discussed and allows the audience to see the bigger picture.
2. **Creates Continuity:** By referencing a prior moment, the speaker can build a narrative thread that connects past, present, and future. This continuity helps the audience follow the speaker's logic and understand how past events or decisions led to the current situation or message.
3. **Evokes Emotion:** Prior moments are often charged with positive or negative emotions. When a speaker references such a moment, it can evoke those same emotions in the audience.
4. **Strengthens Credibility:** If the prior moment involves the speaker's own experiences, challenges, or achievements, it can enhance their credibility. The audience sees that the speaker has firsthand knowledge or has lived through relevant situations, making their insights more trustworthy.
5. **Engages the Audience:** A well-chosen prior moment can grab the audience's attention and draw them into the narrative. It creates anticipation and curiosity about how that moment connects to the current message.
6. **Illustrates Key Points:** A prior moment can serve as a powerful example or case study that reinforces the key points of the speech. By showing how a past experience relates to the message, the speaker makes abstract concepts more tangible and relatable.
7. **Inspires Action:** When a prior moment demonstrates a lesson learned, a turning point, or a pivotal decision, it can inspire the audience to take action. The audience may see parallels in their own lives and be motivated to apply the speaker's insights to their situations.

A prior moment can be used as a reference point to establish a connection with the audience, illustrate a key point, or provide background that enhances thc message being delivered. Think of it like a rubber band that is stretched in one direction—when it's released, it shoots off in the opposite direction.

CHAPTER 4

Inspire Action

Many people flatline a message so the beginning and end are the same. Instead, create a story arc that illuminates the problem and offers an encouraging and practical solution. For many, that's how movements are started that change the world . . . or at least how a portion of the population think, feel, and act. It's about planting a seed of an idea, nurturing it, and encouraging it to grow.

TAKE ACTION TO ACHIEVE GOALS AND DRIVE SUCCESS

> "Action is the foundational key to all success."
>
> —Pablo Picasso

Just like seeds that are planted in the ground, ideas need to be planted and nourished in order to take root, grow, and mature. Choosing the right method for the idea to develop and take root depends on the environment, speaking conditions, and long- or short-term germination process. Choosing the proper elements to use is a bit of mix-and-match game. What works for one audience may not be as effective with another. Therefore, use the following "seeds" to build your gardening kit. When the time comes to speak, selectively incorporate what you think works best in that situation.

PLANT THE IDEA

Planting a seed to take action involves *introducing* an idea or call-to-action in a way that resonates with the audience, encouraging them to reflect on it and eventually act on it. The idea can be planted in numerous ways.

1. **Share a compelling story** that illustrates the benefits of taking action or the consequences of inaction.
2. **Pose thought-provoking questions** that prompt the audience to reflect on their current situation or beliefs, and guide them toward change.
3. **Paint a vivid picture of a future** that can be achieved through specific actions.
4. **Highlight small, manageable, attainable steps** that reduce resistance and encourages the audience to start moving in the right direction.
5. **Align their actions** to core values, beliefs, or goals.
6. **Create a sense of urgency** that time is limited or the window of opportunity is closing.
7. **Use analogies or metaphors**, like "planting a seed," to help the audience visualize the long-term impact of taking the first step.
8. **Encourage self-reflection** and what might change if they took action.
9. **Challenge or nudge the audience** to take the next step by imagining "Where could they be a year from now?" or "What small change can they make this week to move closer to the goal?"

NOURISH THE IDEA

After planting a seed in the audience's mind, a speaker needs to *support* that idea by encouraging it to grow. Providing outgoing support, reinforcement, and motivation encourages the audience to nourish the idea through their own thoughts and actions. To achieve that *active* outcome, the speaker needs to employ some or all of these tips and strategies.

1. **Inspire with a compelling and clear vision** that audiences can relate to and personally aspire to achieve.
2. **Explain the importance of the bigger picture** and why the goals are not just for the organization or individual, but for the greater cause.
3. **Provide a clear roadmap** for moving forward through small actionable steps.

4. **Focus on simple and immediate actions** that build confidence and momentum.
5. **Make the "abstract" goal tangible and relatable** by sharing success stories that illustrate the journey, possible challenges, and final triumphs.
6. **Use storytelling to create an emotional connection** that supports and drives their actions.
7. **Involve active participation** to increase their investment in the journey and ultimate outcome.
8. **Empower the audience** by providing tools, resources, knowledge, and on-going support.
9. **Reassure the audience** that they have the capability to achieve their goals. *Confidence* is a key driver of *action*!
10. **Encourage a growth mindset** where obstacles are not viewed as barriers but as learning experiences to bring them closer to their goals.

Creating a strong emotional and intellectual connection with the audience creates a fertile environment. Nourishing the planted idea, motivates audiences to take action and achieve their goals.

ENCOURAGE THE IDEA TO GROW

It doesn't matter how good the speech is after the initial idea is planted and followed up with logical and emotional information that resonates with the audience. If they don't *know what to do* or *how to feel* after the speech ends, both the speaker and audience will leave feeling frustrated and disappointed. Concluding with a strong, clear *Call-To-Action* (CTA) encourages the idea to grow.

1. **Use CTAs** to tell the audience exactly what you want them to do, such as joining a movement, starting a project, or taking a small first step.
2. **Repeat the message** so the audience leaves with a clear understanding of what they heard, what they need to do, and why it matters.
3. **Create a vision** for long-term impact that explains the bigger picture, benefits, and purpose.

4. **Encourage sustainability** strategies or mindsets that ensure the idea can continue to grow.

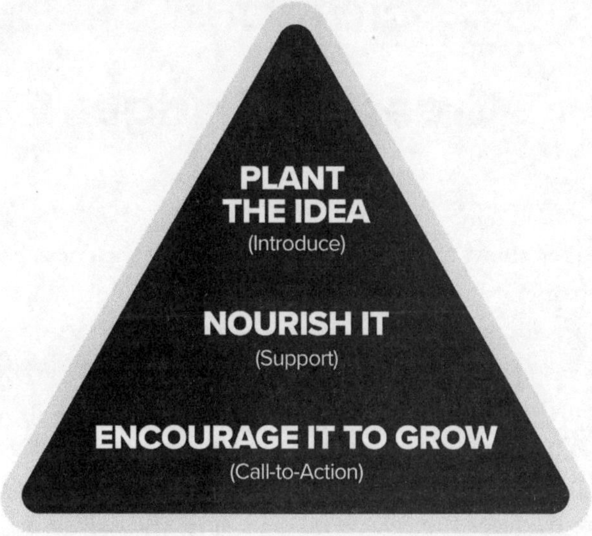

As this graphic triangle demonstrates, the growth of a speech is smaller at the top and larger at the bottom. It doesn't take a lot of time to explain how to plant the idea. Nourishing the message idea with supportive information and actions takes more time. Ending with encouragement to grow the idea may not require many words . . . but expanding the idea from one person to many people spreads the word and distributes the actions.

CHAPTER 5

Create a Bridge

When a speaker allows the listener to connect with the good, bad, and ugly parts of their life, it builds a "Bridge of Understanding" by way of sharing personal experiences. Here's the catch. Being vulnerable isn't always easy. The body likes to put up roadblocks as a means of protection. The amygdala, which governs fear and anxiety, can interfere with a speaker's ability to be vulnerable. When this key part of the brain's limbic system is triggered, it can release unplanned fear and self-preservation emotional responses.

Therefore, you need to "check in" with how you're feeling, identify the "need" of the message, and speak in a manner that "bridges" the communication gap between you and the audience.

BUILDING A BRIDGE OF UNDERSTANDING

> "Understanding is a two-way street."
>
> —Eleanor Roosevelt

YOUR NEEDS AND TRUTHS

Let's begin this section with a process for acknowledging how you feel before you speak, how to stay on track to deliver a successful, purposeful, "need-driven" message, and ways to enhance your truths rather than hinder them.

Your Needs

Check in with Yourself: Acknowledge and accept if you're dealing with any personal issues. These may be big ones that can take an emotional toll on you. Or they may be small ones like being tired, hungry, insecure, ill-prepared, or uncomfortable. It's easy to let emotions get the better of us and build a communication bridge in the wrong direction, especially when life situations overshadow the purpose and need of the message.

Example: If the need of the message is for UNITY and you're feeling insecure, the message will unintentionally be about INSECURITY.

Therefore, before you speak, take a moment to acknowledge your heartbeat, breathing pattern, anxiety level, ability to focus, etc. If you're excited, confident, and ready to speak, more power to you! If not, try to define the root cause of the problem. Are you overwhelmed, anxious, panicked, defensive, overthinking, scared, nervous, pressured, or self-doubting? If you don't acknowledge how you're feeling, unintentional emotions tend to sneak their way into the messaging.

Here are three suggestions for how to check in with yourself:

1. Plant your heels in the ground, place your hands on your heart, and breathe slowly.
2. Tell the problem that you'll deal with it later.
3. Come up with a mantra that frees you from the problem. *[My mantra that allows creativity, freedom, trust, and makes me smile: "This is going to be fabulous or horrible . . . let's see what happens."]*

Your Truths

Monitor Your Truths: Personal issues may interfere with or derail a speaker's ability to be vulnerable. The speaker may hold back, avoid opening up, or present a less authentic version of themself. Instead of embracing the opportunity to share personal stories, emotions, or admitted weaknesses, the speaker may become overly cautious and guarded. The amygdala triggers the fight-or-flight response when it perceives a situation as threatening. And the vast majority of people rank the threat of public speaking as their number one fear!

Here are some reasons and results of self-monitoring truths:

1. **Heightened anxiety** can cause the speaker to stifle their emotions and second-guess their decision to be vulnerable. They may stick to safer, less personal topics rather than opening up and sharing their authentic experiences or emotions.

2. **Fear of being misunderstood or appearing weak** can lead to self-censorship.
3. **Overthinking** may prevent expressing true thoughts and feelings. They may edit or filter their message to avoid "perceived risks," leading to a less authentic or impactful presentation.
4. **Vulnerability** may cause a speaker to pull back when they start feeling the emotional weight and reduce their willingness to share. Or, revert to a more neutral, controlled tone.
5. **Being vulnerable** may open up the possibility of rejection or negative feedback.
6. **The impact of opening up** about personal feelings or experiences may be perceived as too personal, risky, or controversial, even if doing so would create a stronger connection with the audience.

How to share "your truths":

1. **Practice mindfulness techniques** such as deep breathing, grounding exercises, and focusing on the present.
2. **Reframe vulnerability** as a strength, rather than a weakness.
3. **Desensitize the brain** to the fear response by practicing vulnerability in smaller, low-stakes situations.
4. **Gain confidence and trust** by being overly prepared.
5. **Practice** self-compassion.
6. **Accept** that vulnerability comes with a small level of uncertainty and risk.

Acknowledging how you feel so you serve the need of the message while embracing the vulnerability of sharing your truths creates a deep connection with the audience and builds a bridge for personal growth and a relationship of shared understanding.

YOUR AUDIENCE'S NEEDS AND TRUTHS

Now let's flip the focus to your audience. They expect a speaker to be prepared, honest, and *interesting.* Audiences also want to feel understood and connect with the speaker's message. That requires that the speaker "read the room" to see if the audience is engaged or if they have emotionally, intellectually, or physically checked out.

In the mid-1990s when chef Emeril Lagasse was filming eight shows a day of his cooking show *Essence of Emeril*, Lagasse noticed that his support staff and crew started falling asleep after lunch. When a flambé wasn't extreme enough to get their attention, he yelled "Bam!" Not only did it wake the crew up and get them focused, but the catchphrase also became a hit with viewers.

What's the "Bam!" lesson? Come up with at least one good catchphrase you can use to engage or recapture attention. It may not be the word(s) you choose, but HOW you say it. For example, an improviser friend of mine, when a scene got stale and boring, pretended to slap the person she was talking to. I guarantee that woke up not only her improvisation partner but the audience!

Okay, it may not be the most appropriate action to take at a corporate event or meeting. But a physical movement along with your distinct and original catchphrase is very effective. So, play around with it until you find one or more actions and mantras that stick.

Not everyone is good at reading a room, so below is a list of reactions audience members and listeners might have when their need is for an interesting, well-prepared, honest, understandable, and connected message.

Your Audience's Needs

Reading the Room: Negative Reactions

Sighs, yawns, whispering, tapping feet, slouching, rustling sounds, standing to leave, texting or looking at something on their phones, blank stares, quizzical expressions, refusing to make eye contact, crossing their arms, sleeping.

Reading the Room: Positive Reactions

Leaning in, smiling, applauding, laughing, crying at appropriate times, taking notes, making eye contact, raising their hands, participating in activities, asking follow-up questions, nodding their head, mirroring the speaker's body language.

Your Audience's Truths

While there can be hostile audiences, most audiences want you there. That's why they came to see and hear you. And news flash! If you make a mistake, most of them won't know it.

Audiences believe:

- *You* are the expert.
- You're on *their* side.

So rather than letting nerves or self-doubt creep in, feel energized and relaxed knowing that the audience *wants* you there.

HOW THE BRIDGE WORKS

Like any bridge, there are entrances and exits on both sides. Information and energy flows from one side of the bridge to the other, and vice versa. Speaking isn't about controlling the room. It's about feeling the audience, hearing them, and making adjustments to match or enhance their emotions, energy level, and interest.

Did you know that cast members in a play review their audiences each night? Before the show, the cast listens to the audience to gage their enthusiasm. The actors compare notes about the audience during intermission and even after the show. Whether audiences realize it or not, they play a key role in actor and speaker performances. Without an audience, there is no reason to speak. And because audience moods and tones change, speakers have to build a bridge that's nuanced, specific, and relatable.

CHAPTER 6

Rhetorical Appeals

Appealing to the audience's and speaker's sense of credibility (ethos), logic (logos), and emotion (pathos) is not always easy. It may have one appeal missing or sections of it that are unbalanced.

BALANCING THE RHETORICAL TRIANGLE

> "We are what we repeatedly do. Excellence, then, is not an act, but a habit."
>
> —William Durant

Ethos, Logos, and Pathos are the rhetorical appeals. If this sounds Greek to you, that's probably because the philosopher Aristotle was Greek. Back in the day . . . and I mean way back, Aristotle came up with the concept of using rhetoric to defend his personal observations of Aristophanes and Plato and his perceptions of their injustices and distorted truths. He went on to state that if truth and justice are defeated the blame falls on the speaker. WOW! That's a lot of personal responsibility.

ETHOS

Academics divide ethos into two components.

Extrinsic—The speaker's background, experience, expertise, education, and overall character.

Intrinsic—*How* the message is spoken and written.

Since Ethos is a reflection of our history, it's the individual speaker's job to connect with that personal background and share it with the audience. It's the very essence of *why* people listen and take their advice.

Practice Assignment

The next time you make a presentation, record a podcast, teach a class, read a script, deliver the news, or talk to your friends, family, or coworkers, be sure to connect with the overall message.

Example 1: If the story is about **hope**, connect with that story of hope in your own personal life.

Example 2: If the story is about **convenience**, as you speak, remember how you felt and benefited from that convenience.

The defined message is a universal truth that we all possess. The words we say are not as important as why we say them.

***Why* = Your personal history = Your ethos**

LOGOS

Logos is the logical reasoning that supports written and spoken statements. Logos provides specific information like facts, figures, places, statistics, and case studies. Sounds very lawyerly, right? Well, *rhetoric* is the art of argumentation. And the best way to win an argument is to provide data that supports and persuades people to accept and believe your statements and point of view. Logos appeals to people's minds and intellect. It can be simplistic or complex depending on the topic or target audience. Logos provides the what, when, where, and how of the message.

Practice Assignment

"For the things we have to learn before we can do them, we learn by doing them."

—Aristotle

When you say logical information, don't gloss over it. Honor the foundation and purpose of the information. Remember that logos provides substance to substantiate a claim.

***What, when, where, and how* = Logic and reason = Logos**

PATHOS

> "Whereas the law is passionless, passion must ever sway the heart of man."
>
> —Aristotle

In current times, pathos is defined as "showing emotion." The Greek word *pathos* means "suffering." Sixteenth-century actors and speakers used the word pathos when referring to dramatic emotions depicted in a tragedy. At the core of pathos is an emotional appeal to evoke a feeling from the audience. Pathos also lends an imaginative and storytelling quality that can open up people's minds and hearts to past, present, and future possibilities.

Pathos is used to appeal and empower audiences to emotionally receive, feel, and experience the speaker's message in a desired and specific manner. The emotional connection of the speaker and ability to share that pathos should result in the audience feeling excited, angry, happy, motivated, suspicious, hopeful, sad, shocked, etc.

For close to a year, I coached and directed employees at a Fortune 100 company to perform a live interactive stage show for their North American clients. For several months prior to taking the show on the road, I directed individuals and the performance team on how to perform their roles, interact with the video presentation, and demonstrate in real time how to use the software collaboratively with other offices and individuals in different locations. There was a lot of content and information to share. Together, we delivered a high content, informational message that was well staged that incorporated action, emotion, intrigue, logical information, and audience engagement.

After a few stops on the multi-city tour, each of the associates and outside vendors who spoke after the live audio-video demonstration asked that I help them liven up their presentation so it matched the professionalism of the "show." As I refined each vendor's presentation, the energy of the show and the crowd's reaction to their speeches increased. That is . . . except for one holdout who insisted that his presentation be solely logical, straight, statistical data. The end result was a dramatic drop in energy and minimal audience engagement as the logic-only-vendor-presenter sat looking at his laptop, flatly reading the text that was projected on the screen.

The disparity between the performance team and improved vendor presentations and the lone logic-only holdout was vast. So much so that at the final presentation the audience stood up and cheered for the group presentation and all but one of the presenters. Expecting more from that sole holdout, the audience booed, was belligerent, and shouted angry remarks about how boring and ill-prepared he was.

Emotional Importance

Bottom line, emotions matter! Not only is it engaging, it provides valuable information about your opinion and how you and your audience should ***feel*** about the subject matter.

Feelings and attitudes **= Emotional connection = Pathos**

CHAPTER 7

Connecting with the Audience: Checklist

Okay, it's time to prepare for your speaking event. Below is a checklist you can use to acknowledge successes, information gaps, performance inconsistencies, and intentional versus unintentional outcomes.

Performance Assessment

- ❑ List itemized decisions on how to connect with your audience.
- ❑ Reference it often to see if you're leaving something out.
- ❑ Make strategic choices on how to fix sections that don't work or flow well.
- ❑ After the speaking event, do a post-analysis of what worked and what didn't.
- ❑ Acknowledge what worked well that you were pleased with so it can be repeated.
- ❑ Define what didn't land as expected and why that occurred.
- ❑ Identify what needs improvement or adjustment.

After a while, you'll realize what works well and what doesn't, not only at one speaking event, but as a baseline and pattern of what you're comfortable with and the areas that you find more challenging. If you work on the harder sections, pretty soon they'll be your strengths.

PART TWO

TECHNIQUES TO ACHIEVE

Every speaker needs a system to get to the heart of the message and deliver it in a meaningful and impactful manner. It should be focused, credible, believable, trustworthy, and motivational. The speaker should be a storyteller who relates to the problem, delivers solutions, and encourages the audience to feel a particular way and take action to achieve a specific goal.

As a public speaker, voice actor, and performer, I struggled to find the right system to quickly and efficiently achieve these goals. My stage acting method was based on a slow and immersive rehearsal process. Many of the books I read used terms that filled my head with knowledge and my heart with nothing. I attended an acting class for people who wanted to connect truthfully with their emotions. Every week the instructor promised to tell us his system. Three years later he never did share his method. So, I decided to figure out what he and others couldn't explain. After a bit of a struggle, I defined it in 1994 while writing the first edition of my voice-over book, *There's Money Where Your Mouth Is*.

Over the years, I refined and adjusted the Making It M.I.N.E.® performance method through result-based group instruction and one-on-one coaching sessions. I suggest that you stay open to the concepts, *feel* rather than think, be open to specific and general movements, and trust your muscle memory. Save the thinking time for making choices and the performance time for your body to do the work.

CHAPTER 1

Making It M.I.N.E.®: Overview

Making It M.I.N.E. is a method to engage the whole body and imagination to improve communication and performance. The acronym M.I.N.E. stands for Motivation, Intentions, Need, and Emotions. Motivation and Need bookend the message by using the influence of what happened *before* speaking to what is expected from the audience *after* the speech is over. Intentions and Emotions provide an array of actions and feelings that are used *throughout* the entire speech.

PERFORMANCE METHOD EXPLANATION

A speaker uses reactions and memories as a motivation for speaking. Intentions add variety and movement to the message. Acting on a specifically defined need clarifies the message. Emotions lend perspective, opinion, and point of view. Incorporating all four of these elements focuses the message, engages the audience, and establishes authority relatability.

MOTIVATION

There are two types of motivation. One defines a motivational speaker. The other describes how a speaker uses a *reaction* to a prior moment or experience to spark interest and attention.

A motivational speaker shares:

- A personal journey
- A roadblock and how it was overcome
- Life shaping experiences
- Trust in oneself
- An overwhelming connection with the audience

A reactional motivation is used to:

- Kickstart the message
- Springboard the message forward
- Give the message purpose
- Begin a story arc with a specific emotional recall of a good or bad "moment before"
- Share an opinion and attitude
- Attract listener or audience attention

In the Making It M.I.N.E. system, we focus on how a motivation is used to acknowledge a prior event, react to it, and speak in a manner that instantly engages the audience. When a speaker emotionally reacts to a prior event or experience, the feelings are internalized. A physical movement at the exact moment of speaking catapults the message forward, keeping the emotional connection in the body and out of the brain. It functions like a rubber band that's s-t-r-e-t-c-h-e-d as far as it can go. When the rubber band is released, there's an equal and opposite reaction. The information snaps the speaker's message into place and catapults it forward to create an engaging opening and beginning story arc.

In actor terms, "Acting is *reacting*." A reactional spring-loaded motivation inspires resilience and encourages listeners to overcome obstacles with determination and perseverance.

Here's how it works:

1. Connect with a moment in your personal history that motivates you to speak and share your opinion.
2. As you open your mouth to speak, add a kinesthetic movement as you react to the moment before. It could be a nod of the head, shrug of the shoulders, smirk, hand gesture, smile, eye movement, etc.
3. This motivational moment will last a short time. You'll need the other elements in this system to keep the audience engaged and grow the message to an impactful ending.

There are many times throughout our normal day when we see a friend, family member, or colleague start speaking in a unique and specific way based on the moment before. We may enter the room out of breath because we're running late. If we continued to be out of breath and apologized for being late throughout the conversation, then that would be odd or due to a medical condition. That's because the motivation is fleeting and is used to make an entrance and capture attention.

Motivation Practice Assignment

1. Make a list of casual everyday actions and reactions. Then practice using one of them at a time. See, hear, and feel how each motivational choice energizes your message in its own unique way to create a strong beginning.
2. If you don't hear a difference in each motivation, chances are you're thinking too much. Shake it out and try it again without preplanning or placing judgment.

INTENTIONS

Actions and intentions in speech are closely related. Intentions *shape* the way we communicate and determine the *actions* we take while speaking. The tactical approach of what one intends to do shapes how the speaker describes, illustrates, and moves the story along in an interesting and active manner.

Intentions Guide Speech Content: Intentions actively move the story along through actions, word choice, tone, and style of speech. An engaging speaker shares numerous and varied intentions. This adds nuance and variety to the message as different goals, desires, and purposes are expressed. Each intention requires a different action, tone, physicality, and style.

Saying the word "to" or implying it sets up the active intention. Examples include: to inform, persuade, entertain, strategize, resolve, visualize, target, motivate, commit, complete, dream, plan, object, agree, challenge, accept, defend, applaud, disagree, console, excite, etc.

Example: If you intend "to apologize," your hand may move closer to your heart, the words are spoken softer, and the tone is sincere and humble.

Tone and Delivery: A speaker modulates their volume, pitch, and speed to enhance their underlying goal. Based on the intended outcome, the volume gets louder or softer, the pitch goes up and down, and the speed is faster or slower.

Example: If you intend "to assert authority," you might use a firmer tone and speak more slowly to convey confidence.

Nonverbal Communication: Gestures, facial expressions, and body language support and enhance the verbal message.

Example: If you intend "to show empathy," the voice may be softer, and the body language is open and out to the audience to express a connected understanding.

Here's how it works:

1. If you say the phrase "I intend to . . ." gesture with one hand toward yourself.
2. Follow this with the intention word, using the other hand to gesture away from the body and out to the audience.
3. "I intend to" stays the same and the intention words that follow, like *soothe* or *revitalize* or *demand* or *urge* or *mystify*, have different movements and feelings. *Soothe* is soft and gentle. *Revitalize* is upward and energetic. *Demand* is closefisted with a downward action. *Urge* is an inward beckoning gesture.

Intentions are actions used to ensure a win. Coordinating speech, movement, and gestures and wedding them together isn't as easy as one thinks. It takes practice to develop muscle memory.

Intention Practice Assignment

1. Using the aforementioned intention words or other words you wish to practice, move your hands and body in an action that fits each intention.
2. Precede it with an opposite action like rolling your eyes, nodding your head, or shrugging your shoulders as you say, "I intend to."

   Using opposing hands for the beginning phrase and the intention word creates a natural musical pitch and tone difference, tempo change, and focus word movement. This adds clarity and variety to speech.

NEED

Have you ever wondered *why* someone is talking? Does the message ramble on or lack purpose? Does your mind wander when certain people speak? Chances are the speaker hasn't defined their message and culled it down to a one-word "need."

Need = Why

As opposed to intentions, which use the word "to," the need is a single clarifying word preceded by the word "for." It could be a need *for* safety, love, connection, validation, respect, security, understanding, freedom, stability, recognition, honesty, trust, creativity, purpose, relaxation, hope, balance, achievement, empowerment, etc.

The *need* defines the message and provides the continuation of the story. This is different from a more broadly termed company mission statement, objective, and goals.

Business objectives define outcomes and results, such as launch a new product, increase revenue, improve customer satisfaction, or expand market share.

Personal needs are core desires and aspirations that fuel a person's actions and emotions, such as a need for love, security, change, peace, adventure, understanding, success, etc.

In simple terms, an objective is intellectual while the *need* connects to the speaker's emotional core. The more words used to describe a needed feeling or action, the muddier the message. The more defined and culled down to a one-word purpose, the clearer the message.

But What Do You and Your Audience Need?

It takes time to condense descriptive words and phrases into one word. Once you do, the clarity of that "need-word" snaps the message into place. It's the driving force of the message, the connecting throughline with your audience, and the story arc that bookends the opening motivation with solutions and the reason *why* you're talking.

For example, if you feel clear with the description I provided, then my personal need for clarity is met. If you are unclear, then my need for clarity is not met. Therefore, I need to present it better or choose a new "need" that will resonate better with both the receiving audience and presenting speaker.

Need = Subtext
Here's how it works:

1. The spoken or unspoken one-word Need is the subtext that drives the message forward, so it resonates with the audience.
2. The clarity of that Need gives the message purpose.
3. When the core Need of the speaker and the core Need of the audience connect, the purpose of the message snaps into place.
4. The Need serves as a through-line that defines why the message is spoken and how and the message is delivered.
5. The Need acts like a boomerang that is tossed out to the audience and returned back to the speaker, closing the loop with the desired Need result.

How Do You Define the Need?

How does the need fit in with the motivation and intentions in the Making It M.I.N.E. four-step system? The need is the clearly defined one-word driving force to get everyone on the same page and feel a need to take action after the message is over. The motivation is the speaker's prior moment that fuels the need. Intentions are active, engaging, and change throughout the speech to support the need through a variety of actions.

Need Practice Assignment

1. Read the following short message several ways based on a different need.

   Working from home offers flexibility and convenience.
   Reduced commute time can improve work-life balance.
   However, it also presents challenges such as maintaining productivity, managing distractions, and setting clear boundaries between work and home life.
2. Record or video yourself reading this speech six times with a different need.
3. Here are the six needs: A need for fun. A need for recognition. A need for hope. A need for validation. A need for understanding. A need for action.

If you committed to each need choice, your body would have moved in a different way and you should have heard six distinctly different opinions and attitudes. As a result, the audience would understand and react differently to the purpose and subtext of each message. This is why some people say, "The words are not important." In addition to *what* you say, *how* and *why* you speak makes an impact.

EMOTIONS

With storytelling a business buzzword, it's no wonder speakers are encouraged to use personal anecdotes and stories to shape and illustrate their opinion and concept. Emotions capture an audience's attention. Statistics and data, while important, are not as compelling.

Advertising relies heavily on emotion, especially when the logic is weak. Take for example the emotional appeal of a candy bar. We're told that we deserve it, it's a pick-me-up, it's satisfying, it's a reward, etc. Yet the logic of the candy bar is that it's empty calories that our body doesn't need to survive but our tastebuds find enjoyable.

Emotions are the colors of speech. Artists use specific colors and color palettes when they paint. So should speakers. It's very easy for a speaker to get stuck on one or two emotional colors rather than using the vast spectrum of emotional colors that can be painted when we speak.

To illustrate the artist and speaker connection, here's a list of colors and their characteristics.

- Blue—calm, soothing, reassuring, comforting
- Brown—humble, modest, sincere, understated
- Gray—serious, weighty, solemn, formal
- Green—inspiring, uplifting, motivational
- Orange—positive, hopeful, optimistic, resilient
- Purple—authoritative, self-assured, confident, commanding
- Red—passionate, intense, strong, powerful, expressive
- Yellow—lively, vibrant, enthusiastic, animated, upbeat

Feelings and emotions play a vital role in effective communication. A speaker's authority is the byproduct of these uniquely specific emotions, opinions, and beliefs. Life events and personal history shape emotional responses.

Your message has purpose when it leads the listener or audience to an emotional response, so they feel even as they are compelled to take action.

Here's how it works:

1. Emotions reside in the breath.
2. Emotions have movement.
3. Emotional words go up, down, in, out, wiggle, and have inflection.
4. Emotions reflect our point of view.
5. Emotions reveal how we feel about people, places, things, and tasks.
6. Sharing emotions make us vulnerable to those with opposing viewpoints.
7. Emotions connect with people who share the same point of view.

Sometimes our emotions go into hiding and need unlocking. Verbalizing a personality sound that accompanies an emotion can warm them up.

Emotions Practice Assignment

1. Take a moment to read each of the words below.
   - Surprised
   - Hopeful
   - Smug
   - Happy
   - Sad
   - Determined
2. Add a whimper, sigh, growl, gasp, laugh, or another emotional sound prior to saying each word.
3. Make a mental note of how the breath is used and of the action and direction each word takes.

CHAPTER 2

Making It M.I.N.E.®: Performance Application

The Making It M.I.N.E. method can be applied in many ways.

- **M = Motivation**: Kickstart the message with a reaction to the past and movement toward the present.
- **I = Intentions**: Provide action, variety, and clarity.
- **N = Need**: Define the message.
- **E = Emotions**: Add a point-of-view, feelings, and opinion.

Now, let's drill down a bit more on how the Making It M.I.N.E. methodology works and can be applied.

MOTIVATION: KICKSTART YOUR MESSAGE

Openings and closings are the hardest parts of any speech or performance. Motivations in the M.I.N.E. system establish an emotional and imaginative pre-life that fuels the story. But that's not all you need to grab an audience's attention. Here are additional ways to kickstart your message. Each choice requires an awareness of the audience's need, problem or expectation, "moment before" experience, and active movement on or before the first word is spoken to charge the opening and instantly focus attention.

Use the script, structure, and format to create a captivating opening

- Make a bold statement.
- Ask a question.
- Set the scene.
- Present a problem or challenge.
- Open with a quote.
- Tell a captivating story.
- Say something humorous.
- Refer to a current event.
- Use the motivation "moment before" problem to fuel the opening.

Acknowledge the issue, problem, or "elephant in the room"

- A strong opening begins before you speak.
- Identify the problem.
- Take a moment to visualize and recall the problem so you see, hear, and feel it.
- Imagine how your audience will connect and respond.
- Emotionally react to the problem.
- Use the problem as a springboard to actively empowered speaking.

Physically react to the problem

- Nod or shake your head.
- Shrug your shoulders.
- Smile.

- Look up, to the side, or roll your eyes.
- Point, gesture, or acknowledge the location of a visual object, person, location, or scene.
- Make eye contact with the person, group, audience, or imagined person.
- Use an inviting gesture to bring the audience into *your* world.

Shift from the problem to the solution

- Establish your authority.
- Create a story arc as you react and feel.
- Share your "problem to solution" opinion.
- Change speaking tone and attitude when shifting from the opening to the solutional message.
- Use a different physical action, preferably from one side of body to the opposite side, to define the message shift.

Begin with a physical movement

- Find a unique and interesting way to make an entrance.
- Acknowledge and react to the opening music, audience, room noise, or sound effect.
- Refer to a real or imagined visual display or screen.
- Hold up a physical or imaginary object, product, or prop.
- Ground yourself with a physical movement or gesture to get out of your head and into your body.

Remember that your audience is in the middle of their day. It's your job to bring them into your world, share information that compels them to listen, and encourages them to stay actively involved in your message. Use these attention-grabbing techniques in podcasts, meetings, presentations, voice-overs, announcements, and other forms of speech communication.

Incorporating motivation into a speech can transform it from a mere presentation of information to a powerful tool for inspiration, empowerment, visualization, authority, and positive change.

INTENTIONS: PROVIDE ACTION, VARIETY, AND CLARITY

Authentic speakers don't just say words, they embody them with meaningful gestures and movements. An intentional eye-widening, head nod, shoulder shrug, or handshake actively illustrates an intention, making the message more engaging and impactful. Such an approach turns speakers into true performers, painting vivid pictures with their words and actions.

Noun Intentions versus Verb Intentions

Nouns Show a Location: A noun intention gesture that focuses on a person, place, or thing should naturally guide attention toward that stationary location. If the noun moves, like an airplane or a runner, then the gesture should replicate that forward, backward, up, down, circling, or swirling movement.

Verbs Have Action: Due to the dynamic movement, verb intentions should reinforce and bring to life each action it represents when describing or demonstrating that word or phrase.

Body and Voice Coordination

It's very common for speakers to focus on the audience *seeing* them. When that's the case, movements and gestures may be in the spaces between the words rather than as the intention words and phrases are spoken. If the audio is lifted from that performance, the visual impact is lost and the spoken words may not be as engaging. For visual *and* audio impact, intention gestures should be coordinated with the spoken words.

Below are a few mouth and movement self-checks.

Locate the verb action in the sentence. In the following example, it's the word "waiting": "I'm waiting to go into the office." There are two opposing actions to choose from based on attitude and urgency. If patiently waiting, the muscles may relax and slouch downward when you say the word "waiting." If anxious and annoyed, the muscles may tense and tighten up. Try physicalizing these two actions! Say the example sentence both ways (relaxed and tense), changing the physical muscle action only on the word "waiting." If your action and speech are coordinated, you should hear a clear difference in how each of these opposing movements change the voice attitude and opinion.

A noun intention draws focus to a location when that's the most important detail. Let's use this sentence: "I'll meet you at the store." Based on your location, you may point down the street, behind you, at the ground, or even upward if the store is located on a higher level. Now, say that sentence four ways, pointing to a different location (in front, behind, down, and up) each time you say "at the store." Gesturing to a specific location establishes the speaker's authority or knowledge and encourages the listener's visualization and memory. Next, say that sentence again and don't gesture. Could you hear the attitude difference when the store's location was no longer the primary focus?

Here's a curveball. What if a noun has a shape? Without using your hands, describe a spiral staircase. This may test your vocabulary and descriptive word choices! Now, on the word "spiral" use your index finger to demonstrate the cylindrical spiral shape. Stop the circular movement and leave your finger still and in the same position when you say "staircase." That one-word movement draws focus to "spiral," or the *type* of staircase. (Intention: Define.) If you use the circular movement on both words "spiral staircase," the noun intention is different. (Intention: Clarify)

Word Emphasis Chart

For intentions to be effective, they need variety. Below is a chart of thirteen actions you can make with your head, face, shoulder, foot, or hand.

WORD EMPHASIS CHART

●	=	**firm, crisply stated word said in a short, staccato manner**
Λ	=	**raise the pitch of a single word up and down to add focus**
V	=	**lower the pitch of a single word down and up to add focus**
∿∿∿	=	**add vocal interest to a word or phrase by wavering the sound or adding a haze**
——	=	**stretch out a key word**
( )	=	**parenthetical statement to be dismissed quickly or spoken as a secret**
⮧	=	**dip the pitch down and speed up the tempo on a phrase or sentence**
ʅ	=	**hook the listener in by using high, low, medium or low, high, medium musical notes**
↗	=	**arrow the pitch of the phrase or sentence upward**
↘	=	**arrow the pitch of the phrase or sentence downward**
/	=	**beat or intention change**
//	=	**transition**
W	=	**separate the three parts of the sentence—statement, action, and connecting statement—by adding three melodic shifts**

The single and double slashes at the bottom of the chart are for timing breaks and emotional shifts. If you have a script, you may want to use some of these markings on keywords or phrases. You may also substitute emojis that represent similar movements and word emphasis.

Adding Melody and Word Focus

Intentions become active in a variety of ways—muscle movement, facial expressions, and gestures. Active noun and verb intentions enhance and clarify speech.

If you want to practice intentions and corresponding movements, check out my interactive app: **Adding Melody to Your Voice—Speech Improvement Instruction and Workout**.

NEED: DEFINE THE MESSAGE

In contrast to intentions that change often, the *need* remains the same throughout the message. Choosing that one-word purpose for speaking is the most important component of any speech or dialogue. A singular specific need should resonate with both the speaker *and* the audience, uniting them in a shared cause, belief, and response. The need provides the continuation of the message, or "moment after," so the audience not only hears the words but feels the message and wants to take the next actionable steps.

Need = What the message gives the audience

Linking Need to Motivation

A prior event or experience jumpstarts the message. That beginning motivational moment needs a hook to propel the message to the end and beyond. The defined one-word need creates this story arc and continuous throughline. Once the logical word choice drops into the speaker's heart and gut, the message snaps into place as physicality, tonality, tempo, and emotions adjust accordingly.

Much like a boomerang, the speaker throws the "need" message out and the audience accepts that need and then returns that fully realized and fulfilled "need" back to the speaker. This is why finding the right need is so important. A need that doesn't resonate with the audience falls flat and the overall goal of the speech is not achieved.

Selecting the right need must relate to personal, emotional, social, or physical aspects of life. Rather than speaking solely about a product or service, get to the heart of *why* people need something to make their lives easier. The need can either be spoken aloud or implied in the subtext.

Basic Needs: Food, Water, Sleep, Air, Clothing, Shelter.

A speaker's best laid plans may be upended by basic fundamental needs. Most likely you've experienced this when you were hungry and couldn't concentrate or were about to speak and needed water. Basic needs must be met before higher-order needs can be pursued.

Higher-Order Needs: Safety, Love, Connection, Affection, Validation, Respect, Security, Belonging, Understanding, Trust, Freedom, Stability, Independence, Companionship, Acceptance, Recognition, Comfort, Encouragement, Growth, Appreciation, Health, Privacy, Support, Peace, Confidence, Autonomy, Fulfillment, Balance, Attention, Achievement, Hope, Self-Expression, Empowerment, Control, Relaxation, Honesty, Joy, Purpose, Creativity, Justice, Simplicity, Dependability, Change.

A few of the needs listed above, while genuine, are difficult to play. When that's the case, drill down more to get to the core of the message. Need-driven speaking is the result of asking a lot of "what?" and "why?" questions until the root-meaning of the message is revealed. The speaker should experience a visceral reaction to the need that shapes communication, affects relationships, and forms a foundation of human interactions and decisions.

For example, how do you feel when the need is for health or privacy? Is it an external thought or an internal feeling? While these are common needs, the reason why these needs are important will be different based on each person's situation. The underlying reason for the umbrella-need for health may be a personal need for freedom, independence, stability, joy, purpose, etc.

While your mind may come up with a correct need, you must listen to your body's reaction to the need for it to be truly purposeful and impactful. Remember, it's not what the need is . . . it's what the need reciprocally gives you and your audience.

Empowering the Need

Since we're all unique and have different life experiences, each person's need choice may be different. Let's explore this using a short script for this made-up product.

> NeuraLens is a sleek, wearable headset that enhances focus and productivity by seamlessly integrating real-time data with your natural vision. Let's say that you're writing a speech on your computer, NeuraLens displays personalized insights, reminders, and notifications directly into your field of view without disrupting your workflow.

Why would you need this product? In other words, what does this product equal for you? Here are three examples of why people would need this product.

NeuraLens = Freedom
NeuraLens = Convenience
NeuraLens = Achievement

Personal Need Versus Message Need

Our personal need in the moment and the message's need may conflict. This is especially true when a person is nervous, distracted, or doesn't feel prepared.

Personal Need	Message Need
Safety	Understanding
Escape	Encouragement
Control	Freedom
Acceptance	Achievement

You can re-channel your personal need by integrating it into the opening motivation and empowering the message need. The speaker can also check in with themself, acknowledge the need discrepancy, put their personal need aside for the moment, and power forward with the message need.

A business associate used to talk to his personal "needy self" before giving a speech. Imagining that his problem was sitting in the car passenger seat, he told his personal need that he would be back for it later. Then, he closed the car door, let out a sign of relief, and walked into the building. When he returned to his car and opened the door, his personal need was waiting for him and flowed back into his body.

If you've ever planned a party or small gathering of friends, you undoubtedly know who you *want* to invite, who you *have* to invite, and who you *won't* invite. Instinct and experience guide those choices, yet we seldom express a tangible need word for those decisions. The underlying need may be for peace, ease, or fun. Certain individuals in a particular setting may disrupt that chi.

Story arc = Motivation to need

Even though the M.I.N.E. acronym forms a word, the order for preparing and delivering a speech should actually be this way:

1. **Motivation**: Establish the preexisting problem or moment before.
2. **Need**: Select one word that clarifies the message and propels it forward.
3. **Intentions & Emotions**: Sprinkle actions, point-of-view, and feelings throughout to support the story arc from beginning to end.

EMOTIONS: POINT-OF-VIEW, FEELINGS, AND OPINION

Your POV, feelings, and opinions matter, not only in Making It M.I.N.E. but whenever you speak. Physicality and movements make a dramatic difference in how communication is heard, seen, and accepted. Here are some tips and practice assignments for relating to others when you speak, make a presentation, record a podcast, talk on the phone, record your voice, or appear on-camera.

BODY, POSTURE, AND VOICE

Confidence

Our shoulders tell a lot about ourselves. They slump when we're exhausted, shrug when we don't know something or don't care, and tense up and rise when we're in a stressful situation. Each of these physical movements has a history. Our history. Our story with thoughts and images buried inside. Being aware of how you stand and the attitude that corresponds with it is a powerful communication tool.

Confidence is a way of conveying trust as an authority in whatever area of expertise you excel.

If you want to improve yourself in this area, take a moment to stand with your shoulders squared off, as if talking to a person or camera. Relax the shoulders and drop them down. Breathe in slowly and look straight ahead.

Practice Assignment

Select something to read or an upcoming speech. Record or video yourself speaking with slumped or stooped shoulders. Then, try it again with your shoulders squared off, relaxed, and down. Settle your breath and smile gently. Play both recordings back and analyze what you heard or saw. Could you hear more confidence in your voice when you read it the second time with your shoulders relaxed and down? If not, try this exercise again. I have confidence in you!

Authority and Pride

Have you ever noticed how a person stands straighter and the shoulders arch back when given a compliment? Or, how a person may be encouraged to stand tall and be proud. You can use these exact physical movements to enhance visual and auditory impact.

Okay. I'll warn you right now. The directions I'm about to give you may sound similar to what a parent or teacher might have told you when you were growing up.

- Stand up straight.
- Pull your shoulders back.

- Hold your head high.
- Smile; wipe that frown off your face.

Practice Assignment

Stand in front of a mirror or video and record yourself as you act like a blossoming flower. Hunch your shoulders, lower your head, and hold your hands together in front of you. Then open up your body and morph into the pride position by raising your head, standing straighter, smiling, and widening your hand positions away from your body so the fingers extend forward and to the sides of your hips in a V-shape.

To develop muscle memory, repeat this transition a few times. The closed flower position is the "before moment" or "problem." The open flower is the position of "pride." Use the deflated body posture prior to going into an important meeting, when you're about to give a speech or presentation and are backstage and out of view of the audience, or prior to recording. This adds history and movement to your message. Play around with the size and shape of your "flower" transformation. Listen to the different degrees of pride in your voice when you move your shoulders further back, hold your head higher, and stand taller.

Heartfelt

Emotions draw focus to different body locations. Confidence is projected through a straight back and strong chin position. For pride, it's the muscle strength and placement of the shoulder blades. Heartfelt has a more obvious focus . . . the heart. If nurturing, add an additional heart focus with one hand closer to the body, as if it's a hug, and the other hand on the heart.

Let's take a moment to get warm and fuzzy with a pretty amazing trick.

- Place both hands on your heart and gently press.
- Breathe in and out slowly.
- After a few moments, you should feel your body calm down, relax, and center on the heart.

If you are giving a speech, you can do this exercise as prep before speaking. Then, keep your gestures at heart level until you need to switch emotions.

You'll hear your voice change as you move your hands out of the heart location. For example, from the heart area to shoulders down, confidence; to shoulder blades together, pride.

Practice Assignment

Record yourself speaking extemporaneously or reading a couple paragraphs of any written material. See if you hear a difference in your voice when you read the copy and place both hands on your heart, drop one hand, and drop the other hand from that area. Then, return both hands to the heart; keep your two thumbs on your heart but lift the fingers off, and lift your thumbs an inch away from your heart. You should hear an amazing difference in all six of those locations.

Attitude and Opinion

Attitude often demonstrates a bit of cocky, sarcastic, and ironic history that we use regularly when talking to friends and family. But where does it go when we talk to strangers? Weren't we told to wipe that smirk off our face when we were younger?

Having an attitude means having an *opinion* about what you're saying and the person you are talking to. Attitudes commonly used with friends and family members are cocky, sarcastic, and ironic. While to strangers and people we just met we are typically neutral and devoid of attitude. It somehow seems inappropriate or even counterintuitive to add these familiar attitudes to people we're not close to. Why do we give our friends and family members attitude and strangers none? It's because our shared experiences and history together provide permission to speak that way. Let's face it; we've all done stupid things that we tease others about and vice versa. That's what relationships are built on . . . the good, the bad, the awkward, and the embarrassing.

So, how do we add history, opinion, and attitude to a script or presentation about information or people that we're not close to? Let's take a moment to find out how.

Going back to our school years, especially the rebellious middle school days, we often talked to the person behind us when it was inappropriate to do so. Thinking we were fooling the teacher, we would angle our head or shoulders in the direction of the person behind us so we could hear what our friend had to say. When the teacher called us out for talking in class, we squared our shoulders to the front of the room and faced the teacher to appear attentive.

Over the years, I realized that when people had a cocky, smug, arrogant, or ironic attitude, they *angled* their body rather than squared off their shoulders.

If you talk with your shoulders squared off, you'll sound direct and confident. Yet, when you angle one shoulder forward and the other shoulder back, the mouth develops a smirk, a rebelliousness twinkle emerges in the eyes, and an opinionated attitude is seen and heard. It's our body's way of pushing the attitude out of the neutral zone.

Practice Assignment

1. Think of something that you did that was slightly naughty.
2. Angle your shoulders so that one is slightly forward and the other one is back.
3. Put a smirky smile on your face and say, "How's it going? You look good today."
4. Wait a couple seconds to see if an image or moment in history bubbles up.
5. Shift positions so the other shoulder is forward and the one that was in front is back. Then say, "Yep. It looks like things are going okay for you today."
6. Square off your shoulders and say, "You really do look good."

   Did you feel the attitude shift when your body was angled and how it went away when you squared off your shoulders? There is so much history in our muscle memory. Using simple movements and body positions can access those parts of your personality in all forms of communication.

CHAPTER 3

Speaker's Power Box

If you're wondering what a speaker's "power box" is, think of it as a small stage area that the speaker's hands and gestures stay inside. The power box may be wide or small, tall or narrow, triangular, rectangular, angled, circular, square, or thrust forward. When the speaker's movements stay inside a specified power box area, the message is more focused and impactful. Otherwise, the unconstrained movements and "in and out" voice can distract the audience.

Movement of the hands within a power box location and shape clarifies the message, focuses it, and gives it more impact. When practicing your speech, factor in how to fill the space. Should the movements be broad and wide or closer to the body? Create imaginary barriers on the top, bottom, and sides that prevent the hands from going outside the imaginary walls.

Power box shapes, sizes, and positions can focus the movements, sound, and attitude of the voice. To raise the pitch of the voice, position the hands at chest level. For a medium pitch, keep your hands at waist level. To lower the sound of the voice, keep gestures below the waist.

The width and size of the power box is dependent on the message. When the tone is intimate and subdued, the smaller the speaker's gestures and movements are within that confined area. Dynamic and inclusive messages require the speaker to use a wider and broader area to expand their gestures and the power of their voice.

RIGHT, LEFT, TOGETHER

Hand movements fill the space within the gesture box area. The right-hand gestures to the right, the left-hand moves to the left, and both hands gesture simultaneously. Using these three hand movements rather than a single repeated gesture results in three different musical pitches.

POWER BOX GESTURE "STAGE SHAPES"

VERTICAL STAGE: HIGH TO LOW

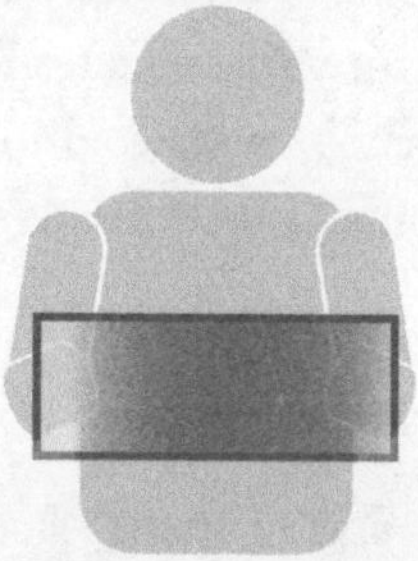

HORIZONTAL STAGE: WIDE AND NARROW

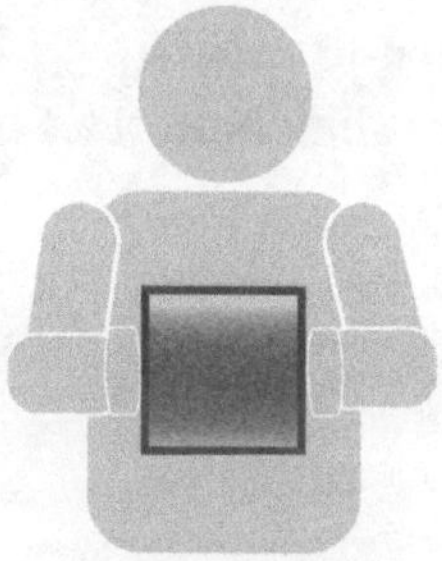

SQUARE STAGE: CENTERED MIDDLE

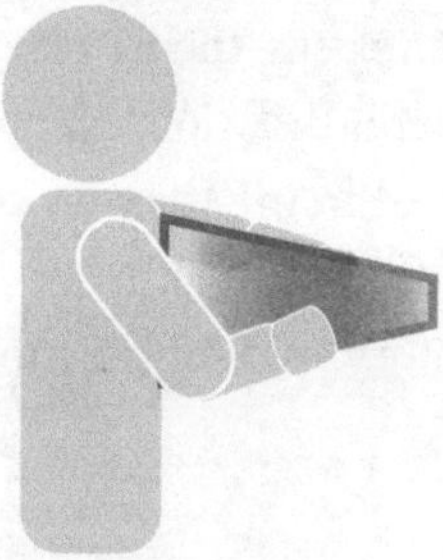

THRUST STAGE: INWARD AND OUT

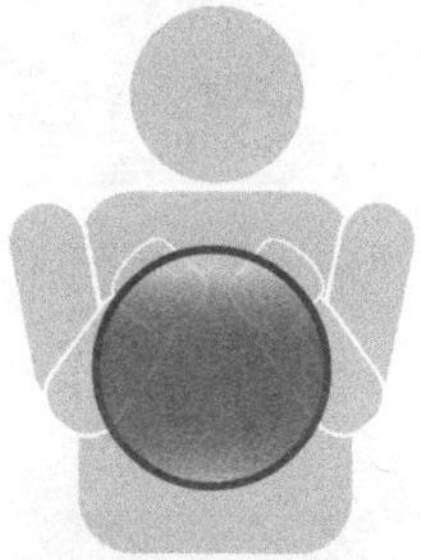

CIRCULAR STAGE: ROUND AND CURVED

TRIANGLE STAGE: SMALL TO BROAD

Take a moment to say something as you gesture with each individual hand and with both hands. Typically, one hand has a higher pitch, the other hand has a lower pitch, and both hands adds strength and gravitas to the voice.

Musically, it's the speaker's tessitura. To quote Merriam-Webster, it's "the general range of a melody or voice part. Specifically: the part of the register in which most of the tones of a melody or voice part lie." The size and shape of the gesture area equates to the same melodic range in speech. The speaking tune may be restricted to two to three musical notes or expanded to two to three musical octaves.

THE MIDLINE

In addition to spatial shape and movement, let's factor in the midline. The midline is the invisible line that runs down the center of the body. When one hand crosses the midline and moves to the other side of body, the pitch of the voice takes on the quality of the other hand's voice placement.

Crossing the hands or any limb across the midline also encourages bilateral coordination. Neural pathways are activated that link both sides of the brain, forcing them to communicate more effectively. This brain-body coordination can enhance cognitive abilities like problem-solving, attention, memory, and motor coordination.

CHAPTER 4

Storytelling

A visual and emotional storyteller creates a three-dimensional world where the listener sees, hears, and feels what you're saying. In other words, narrative storytelling takes the listener on a journey of exploration and discovery, holds the listener's attention, and guides the listener out of purely logical thought and into a creative and imaginative 3D world. But how does a speaker take thoughts, images, and experiences that live in their head and share them with others? Here are three storytelling tips that will help bring your message to life!

1. **Know where everything and everyone is located.** Point and gesture in the appropriate direction to establish where things are in this 3D world. In real life, we gesture and point to places, things, and people all the time. By not gesturing, it's hard for audiences to visualize the location, person, and situation.
2. **Relate to the person you're talking to by having more emotion at the end of the sentence than at the beginning.** If you have more emotion at the beginning of the sentence and less emotion at the end, the attitude unintentionally changes from positive to negative. If the beginning of the sentence has less emotion and a smile or positive attitude is added at the end of the sentence, the message will sound kinder and more uplifting.
3. **Share how you feel about everyone and everything.** Why? Neutral = Bad. Let us know what you like and dislike. Your attitude establishes your authority through opinions and points of view.

SUBTEXT

Connecting with an audience in a storytelling manner requires two additional layers.

1. **Story Subtext:** Utilizing the provided information.
2. **Personal Subtext:** Adding personal memories to fuel the story.

While the written and spoken word are important. The meaning or subtext *behind* the words uniquely shape and mold the message. Using the message foundation, logical information, and structural choices, the speaker layers on a "story-specific" subtext. Imagination, reactions, feelings, and opinions are used to create a story-arc and throughline that moves the information from the head (rational thinking) to the heart (emotional or intuitive understanding).

REAL TALKING TIPS

For additional communication tips, watch, listen, and subscribe to my micro-learning speech communication series: ***Real Talking Tips***.

You can find it on my website ElaineClarkVO.com/podcast, youtube.com/@RealTalkingTips, Spotify, Apple Podcasts, iHeart Radio, or wherever you listen to podcasts.

PART THREE

OVERCOMING OBSTACLES

Remember when you wrote down your five strengths and five weakness in your personal life and as a speaker? In this chapter, we'll drill down on common weaknesses and ways to overcome them.

"The greater the obstacle, the more glory in overcoming it."
—Molière

CHAPTER 1

Performance Pitfalls

It's easy to disconnect from an audience and lose their attention. Maybe the speaker doesn't engage the audience because they're focused purely on information and content. They repeatedly use unfamiliar, overly complex language, industry jargon, and technical terms. The speaker has a flat, monotone delivery. Or, the speaker talks too fast, too slow, too high pitched, or uses too many filler words like "um," "a," and "basically." The speaker is focused on their nerves or an external distraction that prevents them from addressing the interests, concerns, and expectations of the audience. Have no fear, those performance pitfalls are fixable with practice, an open mind, and a desire to improve.

OVERCOMING BAD PERFORMANCES

> "Failure isn't fatal, but failure to change might be."
>
> —John Wooden

Be mindful of these three performance pitfalls.

1. You get in your head and think more about what *they* want than what *you* have to offer.
2. You start strong but progressively lose momentum, energy, and volume that results in a lackluster ending.
3. You second-guess yourself rather than standing confidently behind your choices and the message content.

If one or all of these pitfalls happen, dig deeper than the sound of your voice. Don't be afraid to be spontaneous and real. Allow yourself to dive into the deep water and explore the world outside your control.

- *React* rather than act.
- Allow yourself to be spontaneous.
- Embrace imperfection!
- Remember that perfection is boring and unattainable.
- Be playful and take chances.
- Technique, structure, and knowledge are the gateway to *confidence.*

Be willing to step out of your comfort zone. New skills lead to new opportunities. Push yourself to learn more, change fear into confidence, and add new approaches to your communication skill set.

- Attend improvisation classes.
- Explore stage, film, and voice-over opportunities.
- Sign up for a public speaking course.
- Take singing lessons.
- Start your own podcast.

CHAPTER 2

Change a Negative to a Positive

Some of my most memorable experiences as a speaker and audience member are when something went wrong. I was co-presenting with a male counterpart when he stated something so badly that I stopped dead in my tracks. I looked out at the audience and saw that everyone had their mouths open in shocked surprise. In the next few seconds that seemed like an eternity, the man made a strong choice. Rather than being embarrassed or making an excuse, he acknowledged the faux pas, looked directly at the audience, and said, "Vile. Vomit. Out of my mouth. It's purged. Let's continue."

The crowd and I erupted in laughter, and we picked up where we left off. That moment is burned in my memory, and without a doubt, many of the people's memory who saw it, too.

SPINNING BAD TO GOOD

> "A genius is a man who takes the lemons that Fate hands him and starts a lemonade-stand with them."
>
> —Elbert Hubbard

Transparency keeps the focus on solutions and future outcomes. Pretending that a negative doesn't exist gives it power and creates an unnecessary distraction. Be human. Be imperfect. Be real. That makes you relatable. And a humbling experience can be used to energize and fuel a brilliant performance.

Be creative with your comebacks when something negative happens. Here are just a few examples of how to deal with specific situations. I suggest that you come up with unique ones of your own!

1. **Technical Glitch**—"Looks like technology took a coffee break."
2. **Forgetting Something**—"Appears my brain just went on vacation without me."
3. **Losing Your Train of Thought**—"I was going somewhere with that thought, but I seem to have taken a detour."
4. **Audience Not Reacting or Laughing**—"Saving your laughter for the next joke. Good strategy."
5. **Awkward Silence**—"Ah, the sweet sound of silence. Let's enjoy it together for a few seconds."
6. **Uncomfortable Questions**—"I was hoping you wouldn't ask that, but here we are!"
7. **Unexpected Mistake**—"Consider that a live demonstration of what *not* to do."
8. **Audience Not Paying Attention**—"Some of you are nodding off. I assume it's because I have such a soothing voice."

Humor helps break the tension and reengage the audience. Consider that your secret weapon to get back on track when negative things occur.

CHAPTER 3

Movement Adjustments

If you're wondering if movements and gestures can be problematic, watch William H. Macy in the 2024 film *Ricky Stanicky.* When his character becomes aware of his unintentionally inappropriate power gestures, he is mortified. They are so suggestively bad *and humorous*, that a post credits compilation trailer is added at the end of the film.

So, none of us are perfect, but with a bit of work and readjustments we can stop distracting movements and transform them into assets.

GESTURE PROBLEMS AND FIXES

> "Be sure you put your feet in the right place, then stand firm."
>
> —Abraham Lincoln

While this quote is metaphorical, it speaks to the importance of being intentional and composed in both actions and gestures, as fidgety or unsure movements can undermine one's message. When I work with speakers, they are often surprised at how uncoordinated their gestures and movements are with their words. So, be sure to *practice* the solutions and tips—don't just read about them. You need to create muscle memory, so speech and body movements work together.

Fidgeting: Repeatedly adjusting clothes, playing with your hair, touching objects, or tapping your feet, can distract the audience and make the speaker appear nervous or unprepared. You may want to video yourself, so you know what you want to fix.

Suggested solutions:

- Identify your specific habit.
- Stretch or warm-up before speaking to release some of the nervous energy.
- Take slow, deep breaths to calm your nerves.
- Ground yourself by planting your feet flat on the floor.
- Stand or sit upright to allow good posture to give you a sense of control and confidence.
- Use a trigger reminder, like touching your fingers together or pressing your heels into the ground, if you catch yourself fidgeting.

Swaying: Rocking back and forth when speaking makes it hard for the viewer to follow. When speaking into a microphone, it causes volume changes as the mouth moves on and off axis. The following is a sure-fire solution that I use all the time. To realize how well it works, start off with your feet spread apart. Now, rock side to side. After changing to the suggested foot position, try it again and note how difficult it is to sway.

Suggested solution:

- Place the left foot in the 11 o'clock position and the right foot at 1 o'clock. Slide the right foot into or a few inches forward from the arch of the left foot. *(Of course, you can switch the left and right foot heel and arch positions if that feels more natural.)*

Aggressive Pointing: An aggressive or accusatory finger-pointing gesture can come across as confrontational or rude and potentially alienate the audience. There are a number of substitutions you can use to emphasize a point.

Suggested solutions:

- A semi-closed fist with the thumb up.
- A semi-closed fist, index finger bent, and the knuckle out.
- Slightly curved hands with the fingers together or slightly apart.
- Open-palm facing upward or slightly out.

- Use the side of the hand to make a chopping motion.
- A gentle fist that subtly moves up or down.

Crossed Arms: Folding arms across the chest can make the speaker seem closed off, defensive, or unapproachable. This is also a contagious move if you're speaking to a single person or small crowd as they will subconsciously adopt that same crossed arm position.

Suggested solutions:

- When you become aware that your arms are crossed, change positions.
- Keep your hands at waist level or lower.
- Hold an object like a pen, pointer, clicker, or highlighter.

Overly Broad or Uncontrolled Gestures: Wild or exaggerated gestures that lack clear purpose can distract from the message and make the speaker seem unfocused or unprofessional. If used in a small group or one-on-one situation, it creates tension as the other people try to avoid getting their eyes poked or unintentionally hit.

Suggested solutions:

- Define your gesture area. Using both hands, draw an invisible "gesture box." Start with both hands together at waist level, separate the hands so they are in line with your shoulders, raise your hands straight up to shoulder height, and bring both hands together.
- Practice moving your hands within that rectangular space between your shoulders and waist.
- When speaking, be spatially aware of your movements and pull them back inside the "gesture box" if they become too broad or uncontrolled.

Hands in Pockets: Keeping hands in pockets while speaking can convey disinterest or lack of confidence that can weaken the speaker's authority and engagement as the speaker may appear closed-off or less assertive. And often, once both hands are in pockets, they have a hard time reemerging from that safe pocket space.

Suggested solutions:

- Gesture in a purposeful, controlled, and meaningful way.
- Relax the hands and keep them by your sides.
- Lightly clasp hands in front of the body.
- Place one hand in a pocket and gesture with the other hand.

Pointless Movements: Gestures that don't align with the content or are made without intention can confuse the audience and weaken the speaker's message. Repetitive gestures lose their effectiveness by the second or third time. Walking around just to fill a space and without purpose makes it hard for the audience to follow the message and its meaning. Gestures should appear organic and maintain clarity, confidence, and a connection with the audience so they enhance the impact.

Suggested solutions:

- Avoid pacing.
- Stand still and face the audience when you want to land a specific point.
- Walk during transitions to a new point or topic.
- Use hand gestures sparingly on the most important noun, verb, or modifier.

CHAPTER 4

Procrastination

I don't feel like it. I don't want to do it. I'll do it tomorrow. I can't figure out how or where to start. Look at the laundry . . . the dishes . . . that mess I need to tend to. What's in the refrigerator? Hmmm, that looks tasty. I want to tune out, rest, and avoid doing anything. I'm just not motivated. Why did I say yes? Hours or days later when the deadline looms, panic sets in often followed by a sudden surge of momentum. We've all experienced some form of procrastination and the aftereffects.

WHY THE DELAY?

> "Tomorrow is often the busiest day of the week."
>
> —Spanish Proverb

Most of us are familiar with procrastination, how it can cause delays and pile up responsibilities. This is particularly relevant for speakers who postpone their preparation and practice. But guess what? When we find other things to do to avoid the writing, prep, practice, and scheduling, our brain is still working in the background to try to solve the puzzle of how to start, structure, and deliver the finished product.

When you get caught in the procrastination cycle, create a list of simple tasks. Breaking each section down into manageable bits helps focus attention to one thing at a time rather than the whole enchilada.

Below is a list of tasks you can create to stay focused and minimize procrastination. If time allows, you may want to concentrate on one per day, rather than tackle the whole list at one time, as many of the items require their own set of lists and tasks.

1. **Define the End Goal**: It's easier to articulate the message in a meaningful way when you know the intended outcome and expectation. Start by defining the "need" in one word, as discussed in the Making It M.I.N.E. section. The need you decide on, such as the need for clarity, fun, understanding, adventure, unity, etc., establishes not only the purpose of the message but also the tone and manner in which it can be delivered.
2. **Create a Checklist**: List the main script components, graphics, and props required for the presentation, interview, or recording. To do this, you'll need to break the script or message into sections. A presentation may look something like this: Opening Statement *(graphic),* Problem *(word or statement),* Amusing Anecdote *(humorous photo),* Bullet Points *(separate graphic for each point),* Solution *(uplifting graphic and physical product or prop),* Call to Action *(bold statement with supporting graphic),* Q&A *(2-3 expected questions),* Contact Info *(website, socials, etc.).*
3. **Prioritize Tasks**: Identify which tasks are most critical or time-sensitive and prioritize them. Make a list of the support people *(web designer, graphic artist, writer, presentation coach, etc.)* you need to update information, create deliverables, and add content or support along the way. Give your team a heads-up that you're working on a project and will need their help in the coming days or weeks. That holds you accountable and gives people time to clear their schedules so you can accomplish your goal.
4. **Break Down Each Task**: Divide larger tasks into smaller, specific actions (e.g. "research topic" becomes "find three credible sources," "rehearse speech" becomes "work on timing," and "practice" becomes "coordinate speech, movement, and graphs").
5. **Set Micro-Deadlines**: Assign deadlines for each small task to create a manageable timeline and maintain momentum.
6. **Gather Materials**: Identify and collect any resources, tools, or information needed for the project.
7. **Allocate Time Blocks**: Schedule short, focused work sessions to complete individual tasks to avoid feeling overwhelmed.

Everyone is wired differently for their most productive times and days. If you're aware of your work patterns, try to schedule that time block in the morning, afternoon, evening, or night, depending on what best suits your internal productivity clock.

8. **Start with Easy Wins**: Begin with simple or quick tasks to build confidence and gain momentum. For instance, if you're preparing for a TV interview, refine your opening statement, add clarity and specificity to your bullet points, select a supporting story and pare it down so it's succinct and interesting, or practice your wrap-up and how the viewers can find you or your company, product, and service.
9. **Track Progress**: Regularly cross out or check off the completed tasks to get visual confirmation and gratification and to remain motivated.
10. **Review and Adjust**: Periodically review your plan, adjust deadlines or tasks as needed, and celebrate small milestones.

When you get stuck on the slow-moving procrastination highway, refer to your checklist so your large project feels more achievable and you refocus on making steady progress.

CHAPTER 5

High-Pitched Voice

A common request from people who speak in a higher voice is that they'd like it to be lower. They'd like it to sound more grounded, masculine, or authoritative. They tried pushing the voice lower, but it sounded inauthentic. Or, they lowered the voice by slowing down their speaking speed in order for the vocal cords to move slower.

TECHNIQUES TO LOWER YOUR VOICE

> "The higher the voice, the smaller the intellect."
>
> —Ernest Newman

While I don't entirely agree with this quote, a lot of people perceive that it is true. Placement, resonance, and diaphragmatic breathing enhance and support the sound and richness of the voice. My five-minute *Activate Your Voice* diction warm-up app is very helpful for speakers who want a richer, fuller, and deeper sound. Many people practice along with the app before speaking engagements or include it in their daily voice improvement routine. For best results, take a deep breath from the bottom of your toes, up through your legs, into your diaphragm, and out on the breath as you make the sounds.

When voicing the resonators, create a buzzing sensation on the m, n, l, v, z, ng, ong, and r. Be aware of the location where the buzzing sensation is occurring. If it's in the nose area, try dropping it into your mouth, chest, and back.

Here are additional exercises to strengthen and lower the voice.

- **AHHHH**—Drop the jaw and open the mouth wide. Using your hand as a musical conductor, place your hand at eye level and drop it to the chest area while voicing the sound "ahhhh." Repeat this yawn-sigh sound several times to warm up the voice.

- **MMMM**—Make the "M" sound resonate and buzz. Then protrude the lips forward and back as if chewing the sound as you voice an elongated "eemmm."
- **OH-NO**—Oh yes . . . saying "Oh no" is a way to practice using your lower chest voice. Stick your lips out so they open and close as you elongate the "O" sound in each word. Repeat the "ooohh" several times, lowering the pitch each time.
- **PING-PONG**—This exercise stretches the voice like a rubber band as you shift from the upper to the lower range of your voice. Raise the back of the tongue to the roof of your mouth and hold it so it resonates on the ending letters of PING. Then drop the jaw, lift the back of the tongue to the roof of the mouth, then voice and hold the word PONG. Repeat and hold those two words several times, lingering on the "ng."
- **HUM-NUMB-DRUM-STRUM-CRUMB**—This is my favorite exercise for lowering the pitch of the voice. Elongate the vowel "U" and chew the resonator "M." Begin on the same musical speaking note as your normal voice as you say the first four words. Then, drop the last word "Crumb" down by one note. Starting with the note you just ended on, repeat the first four words in this series and drop the last word down one note. Repeat the process of saying "Hum-Num-Drum-Strum-Crum" on the same note and lowering the last word "Crumb" until you reach the bottom of your speaking range.

Patience is the key to lowering the sound of your voice. No need to make it a big task that disrupts your day. Work it into your daily routine. You can do these exercises while driving or performing household tasks. Vocal warm-ups should be grounding and confidence building. If you find that your voice gets tired or irritated, rest your voice until it feels better. Then, make sure you are supporting the sounds with lots of air so that layer of air can protect the throat. If problems persist, consult an ears, nose, and throat (ENT) specialist.

CHAPTER 6
Disorganization

Disorganization can hinder productivity and clarity, whether in personal tasks, work, or speaking. Is it due to lack of planning, poor time management, too much clutter, or feeling overwhelmed?

Suggested solutions:

- Allocate specific blocks of time to complete tasks or focus on a particular project.
- If a task takes less than two minutes to complete, do it immediately.
- Set realistic deadlines.
- Use the Eisenhower Matrix system for prioritizing tasks.

Dwight D. Eisenhower developed a framework for prioritizing tasks based on their urgency and importance. This task management system helped prioritize and deal with the high-stakes issues he faced as U.S. Army General, Supreme Commander of the Allied Expeditionary Force in Europe during World War II, and the thirty-fourth President of the United States. The Eisenhower Matrix, also known as the Urgent-Important Matrix, continues to be used by people around the world to streamline workflow, improve time management skills, reduce the negative impacts of multitasking, and focus on tasks that are both important and urgent.

EISENHOWER MATRIX

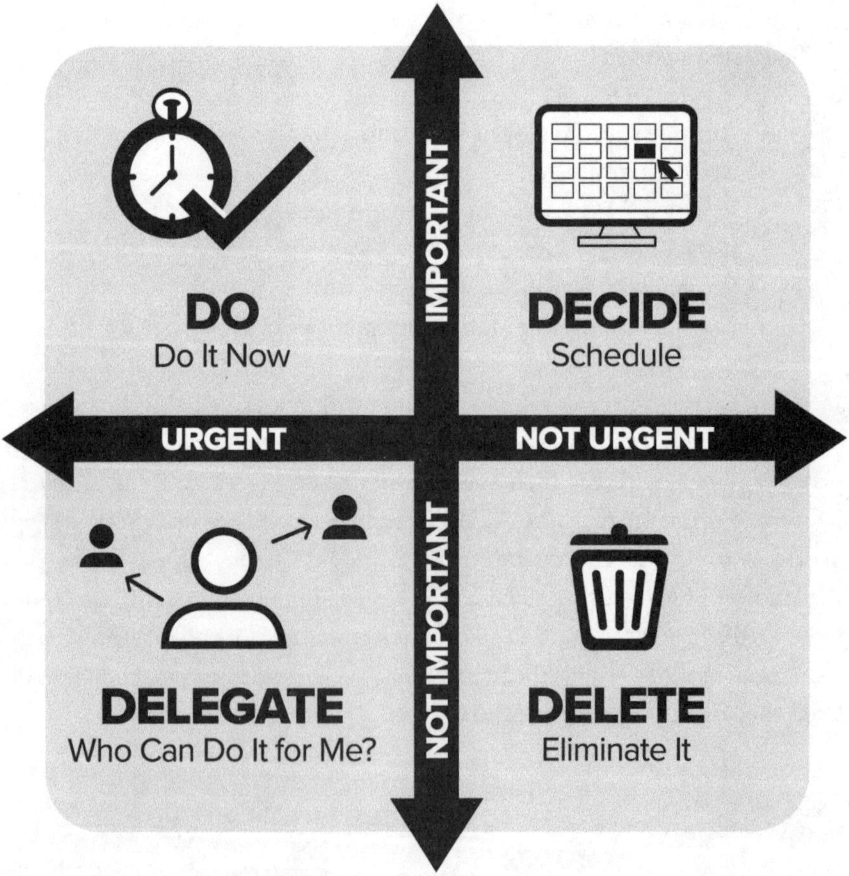

CHAPTER 7

Overthinking

Ever felt disconnected from your audience and the present moment? Have you criticized your performance, gone "outside your body" and directed yourself, or focused on your own thoughts and internal worries? It's easy to be "in your head."

Below are signs of overthinking and potential outcomes:

- **Over-Analysis**: Focusing on every detail, decision, or action can lead to hesitation and second-guessing.
- **Inward Focus**: Internal thoughts can make it difficult to listen effectively, respond naturally, engage with others, and focus outwardly on the audience.
- **Self-Consciousness**: Over-awareness of how people might perceive you may result in awkwardness or anxiety.
- **Overwhelm**: Overthinking emotions or situations can compound anxiety, stress, and feeling stuck.

There are ways to get out of your head and stay in the moment. I've divided the process into three steps—Preparation, Prior Moment, and Performance.

PREPARATION

1. Outline the message listing the key talking points.
2. Boil each key point down into short, direct, and easy to remember nouns or verbs. This "Tarzan Speak," telegraphic, or elliptical style of communication omits nonessential words and focuses on the most critical elements. Thus, it is easier to remember or understand in a quick glance at notes. For example, "In Q3, our sales team had a challenge to meet or exceed

the previous quarter goals. I'm happy to announce today that sales are up 10%," can be translated into, "Team meets goal. Sales up 10%."

3. Create a muscle memory movement or gesture for each of the key points. For example, if there are five points, it might be: two hands out to audience, right hand drops down, left hand finger points out, left hand drops to waist level, left knee bends.
4. Rehearse the key words and muscle movements together as one key point moves seamlessly to the next.
5. When the key words flow naturally in the body and voice, practice adding in the rest of the full message.
6. Rehearse to build confidence in the voice and body doing the work, rather than the brain.

PRIOR MOMENT

1. Settle your breath.
2. Stretch and move to engage the body.
3. Check in with yourself to see if you need to relax your nerves by putting your hand on your heart or energize yourself by jumping up and down and laughing.
4. Tell yourself the mantra you created that calms your nerves and gives you permission to play.

PERFORMANCE

1. **SEE**: Acknowledge the audience—visually present or in your imagination.
2. **FEEL**: Take in the audience and emotionally connect with them.
3. **SPEAK**: Smile, nod your head, gesture, or move as you say your first word. This sudden action will leave your overthinking brain in the dust and allow you to trust the message you purposely placed in your body.

CHAPTER 8

Fear of Public Speaking

If you have a fear of public speaking, you're not alone. Speakers with glossophobia often experience a dry mouth, uncontrollable shaking, and a weak voice. Several psychological, physiological, and emotional factors cause this reaction.

- Fear of judgment
- Fear of failure or embarrassment
- Need for perfection
- Lack of preparation or experience
- Fear of the unknown
- Bad past experience
- Risk is overestimated
- Biological "fight-or-flight" response
- Low self-confidence
- Social anxiety
- Pressure of high stakes result (e.g., job interview, sales pitch, presentation)

Even though I'm a speaker, I've had my share of fearful moments. One such time was when I was hired to provide voices in a loop group (a group of actors who perform background voices in films, TV shows, video games, and commercials) for the movie *The Curious Case of Benjamin Button*. I wasn't a novice in the field, but being from San Francisco I was a newcomer in Los Angeles and to many of the loop group actors. To prepare, I knew I needed to do more research than anyone else to feel comfortable improvising lines in a variety of situations spanning the eighty-five years of the aging-backward Benjamin Button's life. I arrived at the recording studio with notebook in hand and ready to go. So ready, I chose a chair that was closest to the exit door . . . just in case I needed to leave quickly.

I have to admit that my speaking contribution had a rocky start. Fortunately, I gained confidence as my research came in handy and other actors asked to see my notes. Near the end of the day during a pivotal scene, I watched an actor read some specific lines. While it was good, I thought I could do better. So, I raised my hand tentatively and asked if I could try. With all eyes watching my back as the film was projected on a large screen in front of me and the rest of the team sat behind, I allowed my imagination to take over and became the character. After performing the lines, I turned around. To my surprise, the group of actors applauded. When the recording session was over, a few of the actors awarded me an invisible "looper of the day" award.

Why share this story? It goes to show that we all have moments when we're tentative or fearful of speaking in a new environment, among people we don't know, and afraid that our insecurities will get in the way.

Here are some ways to win the battle against public speaking fears.

1. Over-prepare so you build trust in your research and performance choices.
2. Practice in a way that you connect with the words and they feel natural and organic.
3. Start small and build momentum as your confidence improves.
4. Speak to small groups first and gradually increase the audience size.
5. Visualize and focus on the message and the value you're providing.
6. Join a speaker's group.
7. Embrace imperfection.
8. Laugh at your mistakes so your audience laughs with you.
9. Believe that you're worth being heard.

CHAPTER 9

Uptalk

How many times have you introduced yourself in business and social gatherings? What impression does it make if you state your name as a question rather than a statement of fact? If a sports coach encourages the team with a questioning tone, "Let's go out there and win?" it sounds more like wishful thinking than a confident rallying cry.

Uptalk is the upward inflection at the end of a sentence that makes a declarative statement sound like a question. There are many theories on where, when, and why uptalk became prevalent and pervasive. Uptalk works in some countries like Australia and New Zealand, while in other parts of the world it's interpreted as insecure or meek.

For some, it's a process of culturally replicating what they are used to hearing. For others, it may be a speech pattern developed as a result of insecurity, needing approval, or one of the items you wrote in "your weaknesses" list.

While an upward inflection can be used to imply a willingness to listen to other people's opinions rather than just your own, many people find that their ideas, advice, or suggestions are dismissed rather than taken seriously. If that's the case, you may want to reprogram your speech pattern out of uptalk and into a downward ending statement.

Here are five techniques to stop uptalk and land the message:

- Flip the palm of your hand over to face the floor. Then, gesture or point down on the final word.
- Reverse your speech melody by starting in a slightly higher voice and ending down at a lower pitch.
- Press your hand on your desk or thigh to remind your voice to drop lower.

- When saying your name, imagine that it's a firm handshake where the last name corresponds to the downward handshake motion.
- Press your heels into the ground when finishing your statement.

Practice Assignment

1. Try each of the five uptalk tips just listed to find the one that works best for you, or if you need to, use a variety of these techniques to stop the upspeak.
2. Get comfortable making a comment and letting it land. That means, ending it down and leaving a bit of silence afterward so the other person in the conversation knows definitively how you feel and that it's their turn to respond.
3. If you're brave, ask a friend or family member to acknowledge or count how many times you use uptalk. Then see if the number decreases over time as you reprogram how you speak.

CHAPTER 10

Fast Talker

While talking fast can come in handy if you're an auctioneer or reading the small print of a medical disclaimer, most listeners need more time to hear and process what you have to say.

Let's explore six ways to slow down your body, mind, and speech so others can understand and appreciate what you have to say.

- Move, walk, or gesture slowly so the speed in which you talk matches the slower pace.
- Breathe in and out slowly a few times before speaking.
- If you feel scattered and moving in a million different directions, put your hand on your heart and leave it there until you feel yourself slow down and get centered.
- Place one or both hands on a chair, desk, or podium before speaking so the nervous energy is transferred to the object.
- Before speaking make eye contact, physically react, and connect emotionally with the listener.
- Silently repeat a mantra to give yourself permission to slow down. It could be: "You got this," "You're enough," or "They want to hear what you're going to say."

Fast talkers may need a little adjustment time to deal with the internal battle and unfamiliar slower pace. With time and practice, you will be able to pick and choose when it's appropriate to talk fast or to slow down. And if someone tells you to slow down, don't get mad. Smile, nod, and let that comment put a twinkle in your eyes that the "slow down, my friend" message is appreciated.

CHAPTER 11

Slow Talker

Are you a slow talker? Do you drag out words or sentences, take lots of pauses, or require an excessive amount of time to get to the point? If so, here are several tips to speed up your speech, vary your pacing, and add variety.

The reason for slow speech and long pauses is varied. It could be the result of a medical condition, stress, regional speech pattern, learning a new language, slower pace of life, exhaustion, or a natural formulation and delivery of thought processing speed.

I'm not qualified to address medical conditions, so let's focus on business and relationship conversational speed issues that result in the listener getting bored, losing interest, completing the speaker's sentences, or snapping or twirling their finger as a signal to pick up the pace.

If you need to talk faster, here are six tips you should practice.

1. Energize the body by jumping up and down and laughing to get the blood and oxygen flowing.
2. Walk quickly to the location where you're going to speak.
3. If it's not a distraction, point your index fingers together and rotate them in a circular manner. The faster the rotation, the faster your speaking pace.
4. Care less. Pressure of perfection and significance can slow the pace. Shrug it off and trust that what you're going to say is okay.
5. Vary your pace. Use an attention-grabbing statement at the beginning, slow down on important points, and quickly throw away information that people already know.
6. Develop your own attention-grabbing signature movement, word, or sound to spice things up when attention starts to wane.

Practice Assignment

Grab a book, magazine, junk mail, or anything with a paragraph or more of words. With your phone or other video and audio recording device, record or video yourself reading 30 to 60 seconds of that material. Then, record yourself again after jumping up and down and laughing; sitting in a different location, getting up and walking quickly to the area where you're going to read; rotating both your index fingers; changing tempo; and saying or doing something dramatic to grab attention.

CHAPTER 12
Confidence

Our shoulders tell a lot about ourselves. They slump when we're exhausted, shrug when we don't know something or don't care, and tense up and rise when we're in a stressful situation. Each of these physical movements has a history. Our history. Our story, thoughts, and images buried inside. Being aware of how we stand and the attitude that corresponds with it is powerful.

SPEAK WITH CONFIDENCE

Confidence is a way of conveying trust as an authority in whatever area of expertise we excel.

Body, Posture, & Voice = Attitude, Opinion, & Authority

Tip: Take a moment to stand with your shoulders squared off as if talking to a person or a camera. Relax the shoulders and drop them down. Breathe in slowly and look straight ahead.

- Newscasters sitting behind an anchor desk tend to arch their backs, place their hands on the desk, and angle their elbows away from their sides.
- Leaders in a business meeting often sit at the end of the conference table to exude confidence, power, and respect.
- Presenters like to stand center stage and take in the crowd by stretching their arms out.
- Schoolrooms are typically set up with the teacher's desk positioned to see all the students. When a student slumps in the chair, the teacher often calls that person out and suggests that they sit up.

Our confident attitude history begins with shoulders straight and squared off to the listener.

Practice Assignment

Select something to read. Record or video yourself reading it with slumped or stooped shoulders. Then, read it again with your shoulders squared off, relaxed, and down. Settle your breath and gently smile. Play both recordings back and analyze what you heard or saw. Could you hear more confidence in your voice when you read it the second time with your shoulders relaxed and down? If not, try this exercise again. I have confidence in you!

PART FOUR

ADAPTING TO SPECIFIC AUDIENCES

This information comes from decades of practical application in either performing or coaching people in a variety of speaking jobs and situations. The following techniques apply to times when you need a specific kind of action, response, or change in direction. Most often, they involve speaking with purpose using the *power of suggestion* rather than *demand*. This is the foundation of advertising and commercials used for decades to persuade us to buy into an idea, service, or product.

> **"Advertising isn't a science. It's persuasion. And persuasion is an art."**
>
> **—Bill Bernbach, advertising creative director and co-founder of Doyle Dane Bernbach, Inc.**

CHAPTER 1

Three Ways to Engage the Audience

Speakers have three basic audience engagement choices:

1. Speaking *AT*
2. Speaking *TO*
3. Speaking *WITH*

These three speech engagement styles are based on the *relationship* with the audience.

1. AT is direct and unapproachable.
2. TO is direct with emotion and empathy sprinkled in.
3. WITH is a dialogue with an individual or group.

All three styles are valid speaking choices based on the speaker's job and relationship with the audience and work situation. We'll dive into specific jobs in a moment, but first let's review the reasons why and when a speaker might use one or more of the performance engagement choices.

SPEAKING AT

Speaking *at* someone creates a distance or barrier between the speaker and listener. There's little or no room for discussion or compromise. It's authoritative information that is expected to be received at face value and acted on as directed. Often, the speaker believes they are superior, more informed, or of a higher status level.

A few cases where the direct "speaking at" style is used include:

- Police commands
- Military orders
- GPS voice navigation
- Dispatchers
- Public service announcements

SPEAKING TO

Speaking *to* someone is a more casual, authoritative style. The intention is to share and receive information and ideas. There's a proper, businesslike distance between the speaker and listener.

Ways that the casual authoritative "speaking to" style is used include:

- Assigning a chore to a family member
- Teaching
- Training
- Sales and marketing
- Feedback and reviews
- Meetings
- Team collaboration
- Networking
- Negotiations
- Reporting

SPEAKING WITH

Speaking *with* someone creates a real or implied dialogue with the listener. There's a shared familiarity with the people, location, and situation. Speaking with an individual or group promotes active listening, empathy, and imagination. It allows the audience to be *in* the story rather than observing from a distance.

"Speaking with" the audience includes:

- Storytelling
- Personal relationships

- Metaphors and analogies
- Humor
- Drama
- Movements that convey meaning beyond the words

So, as we explore how to *Speak to Achieve* in these various jobs and situations, consider your audience and the best way to communicate with them. The more familiar you are with the material and your audience . . . the more acting skills you may need.

CHAPTER 2

Interview Tips, Techniques, and Trends

New trends in interviewing, particularly in podcasts, media, and business settings, reflect changes in technology, audience preferences, and social dynamics. Some of the most notable interview trends include:

1. **Shorter, Snackable Content** with bite-sized interviews.
2. **Conversational, Authentic Styles** where both the host and guest share personal stories and real-life challenges.
3. **Video Interviews and Live Streaming** that enable live audience Q&A and instant feedback.
4. **Interactive Audience-Driven Interviews** where audiences submit live questions or participate in polls.
5. **Hybrid or Remote Interviews** over video conferencing platforms and apps.
6. **Deep Dives and Long-Form Conversations** that can last one to three hours.
7. **Narrative-Driven Interviews** that combine the conversation with broader story arcs, sound design, and multimedia elements to make the experience more immersive.
8. **Cross-Platform Interviews** that repurpose companion content on social media, blogs, newsletters, YouTube, transcripts, or behind-the-scenes insights to extend the life and reach of the interview.
9. **Co-creating Content with Guests** for a more collaborative and dynamic final product.

10. **Using Visuals and Graphics** to highlight key moments or emphasize data points, especially for more educational or technical topics.

There are so many variables for interacting with individuals and audiences. The voice, body language, gestures, and visual focus changes with all of them. Let's explore the various applications now.

CHAPTER 3
Business

In a business setting, speaking with confidence and moving with intention ensures that you appear credible, composed, and professional, which is key to making a strong impression.

ARMS AND HANDS

What the heck do you do with your hands?! It's amazing how easily the arms become disconnected from the body when in the pressure cooker of speaking in front of people. Hands are powerful tools for expressing emotions and reinforcing verbal communication.

Common body language mistakes include:

- **Dead Arms**: A person appears passive or disengaged when their arms drop lifelessly by their sides.
- **Finger Tugging or Fidgeting**: This distracting movement draws focus and projects nervousness.
- **Crossed Arms**: Unintentionally, this body position often signals defensiveness, disengagement, or resistance.
- **Pointing "the gun"**: Using the index finger to directly point at people can feel domineering, threatening, or disrespectful.
- **Handcuffed**: Hands locked behind the back can project an arrogant, unapproachable, cold, or guarded demeanor.
- **Rubbing Neck or Face**: A self-soothing gesture that projects discomfort, nervousness, or uncertainty.
- **Both Hands in Pockets**: Limits expressiveness and suggests a lack of interest or engagement.

- **Self-Shielding Stance**: Hands low and together in a "fig leaf" protective stance can convey insecurity, discomfort, or self-consciousness.

There are a variety of confident arm and hand positions that are engaging. These positions include:

- **Arms/Hands at Waist Level**: Gesturing out from the torso area is a balanced and relaxed posture that suggests that you are comfortable in your environment and in control of the situation without appearing too aggressive or passive.
- **Cupped Hands**: Cupping hands in front of you implies that you are reflecting on what's being said and handling the situation carefully.
- **Steepling Fingers**: Fingers touching with the palms out demonstrates confidence, intellectual authority, expertise, control of your thoughts, and that you have something important or insightful to contribute.
- **Crossed Arms**: Best used sparingly in a relaxed and casual manner, this position can signal that you're grounded, calm, and self-assured.
- **One Hand in Pocket**: The pocket hand keeps the tone relaxed and controls fidgeting while the visible hand allows gesturing and outward engagement.

Naturally incorporating positive gestures in the proper speaking context aligns verbal speech and overall body language to reinforce confidence, openness, and engagement. While speaking, try to refrain from or avoid repeated gestures. Otherwise, the repeated gesture will cancel out or minimize the impact and specificity of the message.

CASUAL DISCUSSION

Some people feel awkward when talking to a coworker. If you've ever been in that predicament, here's a list of things you can do.

- Before starting a discussion, look to see if the person can be interrupted.
- When it's clear that the person is available to talk, present a casual demeanor.
- One foot could cross over the other foot and rest on the toes.
- Hands could be crossed, down by the sides, one hand on the waist or in a pocket.
- When the conversation if finished, stand up straight and exit.

The voice mirrors what the body is doing and feeling. Create muscle memory that can be replicated so the body and voice know that it is safe to confidently speak with and engage others.

CHAPTER 4

Personal

There are lots of personalities out there. Awareness of the type of person you are and how it stands out, blends in, or takes a back seat to others defines your communication style. That style is most evident at parties and social gatherings. The person with a need for *connection* has a tendency to arrive early and leave late. While someone who has a need for *attention* tends to make a late arrival entrance and leave early.

PERSONAL COMMUNICATION STYLES

- Collaborative and Inclusive
- Visual or Descriptive
- Laid-Back and Casual
- Relatable and Self-Deprecating
- Curious and Inquisitive
- Direct and Honest
- Reflective or Introspective
- Engaging and Energetic
- Empathetic and Supportive
- Humorous or Playful
- Storytelling

Whether you mix and match styles based on context and personality or have a steady and predictable style, how you speak can create dynamic and memorable interactions in casual settings. Listening is a key component in how and when to initiate conversation and respond.

CHAPTER 5

Podcasting

What's your pitch, proposition, or purpose? Whether it's for fun, profit, or an adjunct business, podcasting needs to appeal to an audience. Focus and breadth may be small and specific or large and expansive. I go into detail about the creative side of podcasting and how to use one's voice in my book *Voice-Overs for Podcasting: How to Develop a Career and Make a Profit.*

Here, I offer three different examples of podcasters who strived to achieve more. The purpose is not to gloat about how I helped them, but for you to identify with one or more of their issues and the techniques used to improve.

Referred to as the "Larry King of Podcasting," Jordan Harbinger has an approachable style and knack for securing high-profile guests. Not letting success stop him from exploring new and better ways to communicate, he reached out to me to solve a specific problem: make scripted dialog sound conversational and spontaneous. Some of the terms they use refer to word emphasis, musicality, tempo, and tone. I'll let Jordan and his co-host/producer, Gabriel, describe the process.

JORDAN HARBINGER

Creator, *The Jordan Harbinger Show*

GABRIEL MIZRAHI

Producer & Co-host, *The Jordan Harbinger Show*

We came to Elaine for coaching to connect more deeply to the material in our advice episodes, find the emotional arc of our storytelling, and generally make our show both polished and alive. We also wanted to tap into more playfulness, spontaneity, and authenticity as podcasters.

Elaine helped us overcome the tendency to deliver information in a way that sounds flat, rote, or disconnected. She helped us dial in the emotional tone of our responses, and also encouraged us to find moments of levity and playfulness in otherwise heavy material so we could:

- Connect emotionally to the text.
- Find the arc and rhythm to our episodes.
- Tap into our playfulness and spontaneity.
- Create more silent communication between us as hosts.

A few of Elaine's techniques are always with us when we record—"arrowing" up or down, "hunkering" down when appropriate, and matching each other's energy and cues during handoffs.

> Our listeners regularly comment on how meaningful, fun, and intimate our show is, and how much they enjoy and relate to the stories we tell, both from the audience and from our own lives.

This second interview with "Dan the Produce Man" illustrates the power of a well-constructed story arc and authenticity. Sometimes speech communication comes in the form of a written proposal. When coaching Dan Avakian to improve specific areas of his audio and video performances, he told me a story about a product he endorsed. It was clear that he had a genuine connection and positive history with it. Rather than pitch the potential sponsor on what they expected, I suggested that he change the focus to the product he genuinely believed in. When he sent me the pitch, it was filled with valuable information. One thing was missing: a story arc. I rearranged the proposal so the information and his connection with it told a story . . . much like how he verbally shared his unique experience with me! I emailed the revised version to him and, well . . . I'll let Dan tell the story of how his voice and words worked together to achieve positive results.

DAN AVAKIAN, A.K.A. DAN THE PRODUCE MAN

Podcaster who hosts the Produce Industry Networks *Fresh from the Field Fridays* podcasts and videos on his YouTube and Rumble channels.

> I sought Elaine Clark out because there were things that were bothering me about my podcast. What attracted me to working with her is how real, genuine, and authentic she is. Elaine helped me tremendously by pinpointing specific areas where I could improve and coaching me to achieve those goals and make those adjustments.
>
> Next, I told her that I was searching for that elusive species called "a sponsor," and asked Elaine to help with that, too. We chatted for a while, and I told her about my past experience with Dole when I had my radio show. She told me to write the pitch and sent it to her. She took it, cleaned it up, rearranged it, and made it way more effective. She added in a line from our discussion relating back to my radio days and the characters Bobby Banana and Penelope Pineapple, and how my belief in what Dole was doing was solid and strong. The pitch had a cohesive story arc, history, relationship with the product, and a strong

> call to action. I put the pitch in to Dole and got a response back faster than I expected. They bought a Premium Sponsorship! And I'm tremendously grateful for Elaine's amazing help on that.

Of course, I'd like to guarantee that every podcaster can have that immediate sponsorship result. But having a cohesive story arc where the information builds to a crescendo and strong call-to-action certainly helps. Even when the topic is serious, expect that result.

Pathology is a far cry from tropical fruit. Which is why Dennis Strenk contacted me to help liven up his podcast's coverage of dry (and sometimes gross) medical procedures and to make them more interesting. As he discovered, when information is delivered in a purely logical manner, it can sound flat and detached. When discussing serious subjects, adding levity and personality can feel inappropriate. Yet, that is needed in every interaction. Speaking is not solely about logical information. It's about incorporating logic in the rhetorical triangle of speech so emotional reactions and personal stories resonate with the listener. Gestures, movement, word focus, and message definition contribute to more engaging storytelling. Before long, those learned skills dramatically transformed his podcast and seeped into his personal life. Here's Dennis Strenk's assessment of the process.

DENNIS STRENK

Pathologists' Assistant and Host of the *People of Pathology* podcast

> Before working with Elaine, I often received feedback that my voice sounded flat and lacked emotion. I started sessions with her specifically to work on this, and her approach quickly made a difference. Elaine introduced me to techniques that brought tonality and what she calls "melody" into my voice. Through practice, these exercises became second nature, and the improvement was noticeable—not just to me, but to others, too. I heard comments about how much more engaging and expressive I sounded, which was an incredible boost.
>
> But the benefits went deeper. Alongside a stronger, more dynamic speaking voice, I gained confidence. I found myself speaking with authority, and, surprisingly, I felt free to experiment—playing with humor, or even being a little silly at times, something I never would

have tried before. Elaine's guidance truly transformed the way I communicate.

One of the most surprising aspects of working with her was how much it opened up my overall expression. I became more aware of the impact of my voice, not just in formal settings but in everyday interactions. The techniques Elaine shared are now part of my normal routine. They help me adapt my tone and presence based on my audience, whether I'm podcasting, presenting, or simply conversing. Now, the *People of Pathology* Podcast is #1 on Feedspot's list of 20 Best Pathology Podcasts (https://blog.feedspot.com/pathology_podcasts/).

CHAPTER 6

Presentations

Imagine this: you're standing in front of a group of people. Being nervous or stressed out is optional but not preferred. You have to introduce someone, demonstrate a product, give a lecture, or deliver a speech. It requires preparation, planning, writing, visual aids, and Q&A. The purpose is for one or all of the following: to persuade, inspire, motivate, build goodwill, present a new idea or product. As a presenter, you are the biggest advocate.

PERSONALITY + PASSION + TRUTH = SINCERITY

Personality: Be yourself on a good day in this enhanced speaking environment.
Passion: Believe in your product and what you're making and presenting.
Truth: Trust and believe your message.
Sincerity: Let your sincerity and originality guide your presentation.

PRESENTATION SUCCESS TIPS

1. **K.I.S.S.**—Keep It Simple Stupid. (Not an original idea . . . but a good reminder.)
2. **Talk slower than usual**—especially if you're a fast talker or the environment has an audio delay or echo.
3. **Stay on message**—It's easy for the speaker *and* the audience to lose track of the throughline when too many dangling idea threads and offhand comments are added.
4. **Be animated and energetic**—Involve your whole body and voice to support the message. Be sure that you're grounded to prevent speeding up as the energy increases.
5. **Embrace your personality**—Allow your inner feelings and outer movements to shine through.

6. **Repeat your messages**—When needed, repetition is a good thing. The *Rule of 7* marketing principles is based on repeated exposure to increase awareness, recognition, retention, and recall.
7. **Listen**—Audience members are going to ask you questions. Hear their words and message so you can respond appropriately.
8. **Be "in the moment"**—Go moment to moment and don't think ahead. While it sounds simple, it's harder than most people realize.
9. **Think before you speak**—Don't be afraid to take a moment to feel and process an idea, question, or concept. Silence can be your friend.
10. **Create sound bites**—Don't be afraid to add client and product information to numerous sentences, as direct quotes are often taken verbatim from speeches and presentations.

Presentations are delivered in all shapes and locations before varying size audiences. Each one comes with its own set of benefits, obstacles, and requirements. How you enter, command the room, and exit leaves a lasting impact on the audience.

LARGE STAGE

Here are some suggestions on how to use your body, voice, gestures, and movements in a large room or venue.

Opening Moment

When presenting before a large audience, walk to the downstage center area of the stage that is closest to the audience. If possible, avoid standing behind a podium. Square the shoulders to the audience. Position your feet at "11 and 1 o'clock" positions so they point out slightly to the sides with one foot somewhat forward to prevent swaying. This also adds visual interest as the angle of the feet breaks the flat line of the body. With both hands at waist level, gesture outward to initiate a connection with the audience.

Visual Focus

Scan the entire audience. Then divide the room into sections. Focus first on someone in the middle of the room. Then, select a person or group on one side of the room and then the opposite side. Continue to direct your attention throughout the whole audience—front, back, right, left, and center— at various times throughout your speech. You may want to use open hand gestures when you address each person or area of the audience.

Movement

Remain still on important information and look directly at the audience. Walk during thinking moments or during action sentences or statements. Avoid walking back and forth so you always return to the same spot you just left. Instead, add variety by never returning to the same spot and using different locations of the stage. Vary the pacing of the movements based on attitude and content. Lead the audience's attention with a simple single hand gesture in the direction you intend to walk.

Visual Aids

When showing a graphic, chart, or video, look at the audience first then gesture toward the visual display or object. To draw focus away from you and onto the visual aid, walk out of the viewing area, drop your arms, angle your shoulders toward the display, and hold your hands together. Look intently at the visual. When you want to draw focus to the visual display, turn to the audience, gesture with an open, relaxed hand or with two fingers, and guide the audience's attention. When speaking on a large stage, fill the space with intentional gestures that are wide enough for people in the back of the room to see and follow.

Leading the Audience

When walking, guide the audience's attention in the direction you intend to move by leading with an open hand in the direction of that movement. Let the gesture linger there a couple seconds to draw focus to where you're going to move. Then step in that direction.

Strong Ending

To end the presentation, stand front and center and gesture widely outward to take in all the people in the room. Your feet can be in a wider-spread 11 and 1 o'clock position. If appropriate, you may want to nod and smile or give a sign of appreciation and acknowledgment.

Exiting the Stage

Lead the audience in the direction of the exit by lifting one hand in that direction before walking away. Before completely out of view, you may want to give a final wave or friendly gesture to the audience.

SMALL GROUP PRESENTATION WITH VISUALS

Conference Room

When talking to people sitting in a group or around a conference table, take in everyone in the group. Look to the person directly in front of you first, then the people furthest away on your right and left. Next look at the people in between, and briefly address people nearest you on both sides. As questions or comments arise, make eye contact with the questioner, and then look around to the rest of the room to make sure the others are tuned in.

- Avoid shuffling papers, playing with the equipment, looking down at the table, rocking back and forth, and angling the shoulders away from the audience.
- To earn people's attention, lightly touch the table to ground yourself and "own" your space, square the shoulders to the group, and make eye contact with several members. Gesture with shoulders angled toward the presentation display. When finished or to make a strong point, return to the squared shoulder stance, facing the group.
- Whether speaking or listening, avoid melting into your chair and appearing disinterested. Stay in the upright (good posture) position and remain engaged.
- When standing, plant your feet in the 11 and 1 o'clock foot position to prevent swaying. Take a second or two to lightly touch the top of the table to establish authority and ownership of the space. Gesture with one or both hands in the waist high position. Your shoulders should be squared to the audience.

- When showing a graphic, chart, or video, look at the audience first then gesture toward the visual. Angle your shoulders in that direction to guide the group's attention and focus.
- Look at the group when making a point. You may want to gesture using the hand that's closest to the people in the room. When directing attention back to the visual shown behind you, gesture with the hand that's closest to the visual.
- During the Q&A, keep your hands at waist level with hands either cupped on top of each other or steepled with fingers spread and opposing fingertips pressed together. As people speak, gesture to them with a slightly cupped hand to draw focus to that person.
- To end the meeting, gesture outward to take in all the people in the room. Then, briefly touch the table to end the meeting.

TRADESHOWS

As a presenter at tradeshows, the noise level of the event and the exhaustion level of the attendees are major obstacles to overcome. Trade booths are close together, companies announce live giveaways, mascots in costumes wander around, booth buddies corral people into their presentation and sales areas, and attendees are overwhelmed with options and time constraints.

Tradeshow presenters, no matter how much they practice prior to the event and rehearse on location the day before, may encounter technical difficulties with microphones, video displays, unstable Wi-Fi, and electrical outages. While that might require a little ad-libbing and performance rewiring, the main issues are vocal strain and keeping the audience awake and engaged.

Voice Fatigue and Strain

It is very easy to get a sore throat, hoarseness, or even lose your voice when speaking multiple days for long hours. In addition to coming prepared with plenty of water and throat lozenges that soothe the throat without drying it out, vocal rest between presentations and after the convention doors close is a necessity! Conserve energy and disengage from speaking with coworkers unless absolutely necessary. Don't feel bad if you need to sit in a chair and stare straight ahead. Stand up and announce the presentation starting in ten minutes . . . five minutes . . . and one minute. Then, make a big entrance that excites the audience. If you're on a headset giving a live description that's projected on a screen, adapt to the size of the crowd and their interest level to stay and watch or pause briefly to see what's happening while passing by.

Audience Engagement

Attendees are often fatigued and overwhelmed during a convention, especially at the end of the day and later in the week. When they sit down to watch the presentation, don't be surprised if several of them nod off. It's the presenter's job to keep the show active and engaging. When I need to wake folks up, I clap my hands and shout something like, "This is the best part," "You don't want to miss this," or "Check this out."

If the company provides free swag, such as T-shirts to throw out to the crowd or a contest to enter, that tends to energize an audience. When you make it to the end, the next step is to direct the audience to the sales or tech team for more information.

BUSINESS PITCHES

For decades I've coached an assortment of CEOs, CFOs, VPs, and other top-tier executives and teams. Tailoring the pitch to the audience's needs, interests, and goals is crucial for success. In business situations it's easy to rely heavily on data and logical information and leave out the emotional component.

Here are a few examples of how business pitches can differ based on content, timing, and expectations.

- When coaching the CFO of a major media company for his quarterly income and projections report to the board members, his speaking tone remained neutral. While the billion-dollar plus revenue amounts were astounding, it was unclear whether the amount was above, below, or met expectations. By smiling casually on the numbers that met or exceeded quarterly growth, the message projected a more positive outcome.
- I also coached the owner of an architecture firm and her team to pitch cities, counties, and businesses for ADA compliant sidewalks, buildings, and accessible environments.

When pitching to government agencies, each firm is allotted a specific time slot and a limited length of time to make the presentation. We practiced efficient ways to introduce each member of the team, delivering the opening pitch, seamless integration of visuals and handouts, transitions from one team member to the next, how each person would oversee specific areas of the project, deliver a conclusion with the highlights and benefits of working with their company, and exit with time to spare so the speakers wouldn't feel rushed or get cut off before making their concluding statements.

- When adding voice-over to videos used to pitch investors and venture capitalists, I've found that a successful voice is much like an athlete wearing the same lucky socks to each game. If the voice-over supports the visuals in a knowledgeable and easy manner that results in a signed contract, the company that hired the voice actor is likely to use the same voice with the expectations of the same financially successful results.

CHAPTER 7

Speeches

Most likely you're going to have to give a speech in business or in your personal life. Based on the audience, each speech needs to be tailored and adjusted to suit the situation and anticipated outcome. The style of how the message is delivered can be formal, casual, informative, heartfelt, persuasive, demonstrative, entertaining, motivational, inspirational, celebratory, impromptu, argumentative, extemporaneous, oratorical, humorous, satirical, eloquent, raunchy, aspirational, accepting, reflective, or encouraging.

Yet, sometimes speaking situations throw us curveballs that require adaptation. Before a friend passed away, she gave me a passage from a play to read at her memorial service. While it represented how she felt at the time, the text was filled with anger and blame. After many lost nights of sleep, I finally came up with a solution for how to turn this maudlin and bitter story into a loving, respectful, and aspirational message. The answer was: context, lighthearted emotions, eye contact with key individuals and groups in the audience, and the need for understanding! My goal was for the audience not to cry or feel guilty but to smile and fondly remember their friend and family member. I wrote an opening and closing paragraph that reset the terms of how the congregation should listen, and sandwiched the passage in the middle making sure it was spoken with love and respect.

WANT TO BE A PAID SPEAKER?

If you want to speak at colleges, universities, conferences, businesses, and social gatherings, here are some tips on how to build your speaking business.

- Define who you are and what message and experience you have to offer.
- Create a problem that only *you* can solve.

- Title the type of speech solution: Resilience, Overcoming Challenges, Self-Worth, Work-Life Balance, etc.
- Build your own sandbox category: "Design Your Future," "Embrace Change," "The Power of Listening," "Turning Dreams into Reality," "Speak to Achieve," etc.
- Market the problem, not the solution.
- Monetize the solution.
- Deliver value.
- Search and prospect for paid speaking jobs.

As a reference point, school associations often pay speakers on a sliding scale based on subject matter, popularity, audience size, length and complexity of the talk, and . . . of course . . . budget. Some speakers prefer to market an "all inclusive" rate that is higher that includes the cost of the flight and hotel. If you're building a speaker business and encounter financial pushback, you may choose to waive your fees. But never speak for free. The rate you establish is based on your personal perceived worth.

LinkedIn is a good place to explore job opportunities. By searching popular and niche hashtags speakers can expand their reach and target audiences with specific interests. Below are a few common hashtags to promote your posts and locate speaking events.

Industry-Specific

- #PublicSpeaking
- #MotivationalSpeaker
- #Keynote Speaker
- #SpeakerLife
- #LeadershipSpeaker
- #ProfessionalSpeaker
- #InspirationalSpeaker
- #ConferenceSpeaker
- #CallForSpeakers

General Professional

- #Leadership
- #Success
- #Entrepreneurship

- #PersonalDevelopment
- #GrowthMindset
- #CareerGrowth
- #LeadershipDevelopment
- #BusinessTips

Event-Related

- #Conference
- #EventSpeaker
- #Webinar
- #Summit
- #VirtualEvent
- #LiveEvent
- #NetworkingEvent

Audience Engagement

- #Storytelling
- #MindsetMatters
- #SelfImprovement
- #Inspiration
- #Motivation
- #Empowerment
- #ProfessionalGrowth

Niche Topics

- #SalesTraining (for sales-focused talks)
- #WorkplaceCulture
- #Innovation
- #MentalHealth (for talks on well-being)
- #DiversityAndInclusion
- #TeamBuilding

TEDX AND TED TALKS

The goal of many speakers is to present a TED Talk. That requires filling out a nomination form on the speaker-nominations.ted.com website. Then wait to see if you're selected. Speakers can also submit applications to independently operated TEDx events in various cities that are separate from TED Talks. These smaller venue talks serve as valuable standalone events or preparation for the larger TED stage. TED Talks are typically presented by world experts who share new knowledge and research in their fields. TEDx events have a theme that the speaker tailors their talk to fit within. The total length of both TED and TEDx talks is limited to eighteen minutes.

Written Submission: Develop a Compelling Idea

- **Focus on "Ideas Worth Spreading"**: TED looks for fresh, insightful, or transformative ideas that can have a broad impact. Focus on creating a clear, original message that resonates universally.
- **Refine Your Idea**: Articulate your core message concisely and compellingly, answering why it matters and how it could impact others.

Preparing the Speech: Build a Unique Perspective or Story

- **Share Your Experience or Expertise**: Use personal experiences, expert knowledge, or a unique perspective to make your talk both informative and memorable.
- **Incorporate Universal Themes**: TED Talks often address topics that connect with fundamental human experiences, like innovation, resilience, empathy, or social change.

Becoming a TED speaker is a process that requires a unique, refined idea, and preparation. Many speakers network within the TEDx community. Numerous individuals and companies provide valuable guidance and training to speakers who need additional support.

CHAPTER 8

Politics

Style and tone factor prominently in political speeches, rallies, presentations, advertisements, and endorsements. A persuasive political speech needs to connect with the audience's values and concerns, show authenticity and empathy, project confidence and conviction, and offer solutions and vision.

Defining the politician's message into a one-word *need* clarifies and focuses the campaign. Because of the urgency of the election, a political *need* word is often stronger than the need word used in business.

- **"Need" words in politics include** hope, fear, change, unity, resistance, vision, opportunity, freedom, security, accountability, and progress.
- **"Need" words in business tend to include** simplicity, speed, reciprocity, diligence, differentiation, value, improvement, superiority.

A politician should focus on one or two main points and make them memorable. Key phrases and slogans should be repeated so they connect with the audience, can be printed on a sign, and give supporters something to remember, repeat, and rally around.

At big events, politicians often speak behind a podium and read off a teleprompter. Two things to remember in that situation.

- The podium offers protection from outside and can easily be used as a crutch to hide behind or add distance from the audience. Standing upright, using powerful and expressive gestures, and speaking with a strong and persuasive voice can engage and fire up an audience.

- When reading a teleprompter, appear as if the message is spontaneous and not scripted. Depending on the venue, there are typically one to three teleprompter monitors. At transition points, the speaker should naturally switch emotions, gestures, and eye focus. Remember that the job of the teleprompter operator is to follow the speaker, not the other way around.

When speaking into a stationary microphone, stay approximately the same distance away from the mic to keep the sound level consistent. If wearing a lavalier mic, be careful not to unintentionally hit it or place your hand on top of it to avoid creating a distracting sound, audio interference, or muffled voice.

CHAPTER 9

Job Interviews

Positive body language and job interview etiquette are not always addressed by young people entering the job market or long-term employees pursuing new job opportunities. In-person and virtual interviews require specific adjustments to come across as credible and trustworthy. Below are coaching tips I've given my clients to practice and implement in various situations in accordance with each company's unique business hiring practice.

VIRTUAL INTERVIEW

More and more interviews are done virtually. This has its own set of advantages and disadvantages. Virtual meetings are cost-effective, time saving, and provide greater accessibility and scheduling flexibility. However, it's harder to assess body language, eye contact, and other interpersonal skills. Familiarity with the virtual platform, good video lighting and sound, a stable internet connection, quiet environment, and positioning the face and upper body close to the camera minimizes communication barriers and the potential for negative perceptions and biases.

Depending on the type of job, the questions and expected responses will be different. There are companies that train people to answer a set of job-specific questions like: "Why is a manhole cover round rather than square or rectangular?" And others that ask questions about your background, why you want the job, and the value you'll provide to the company.

Listen to the nuances of each question and respond as it pertains to that company. Show passion for the job and an ability to work as a team. The company is the star of the show. The job interviewer is a potential player hired to support the show. If you think this way, it will remove some personal anxiety and nervousness as the focus is not on you, but on the employer.

Smile, relax, appear casually knowledgeable, speak in short sentences with space for an interactive dialogue rather than a run-on monologue, and end statements with a downward and confident inflection.

IN-PERSON INTERVIEWS

After the résumé is accepted and the interview meeting date is set, stress and anxiety can easily kick in and adversely affect employment results. The following details are designed to help you shine in the moment and not let nerves take over.

1. **The in-person interview** begins when you leave your home with the required materials and your list of questions. Allow extra travel time so you won't be stressed. Way too many people have lost the job when they discovered that the person they yelled at, made a rude gesture to, or cut off on the roadway was the person conducting the interview. Whoops!
2. **After checking in**, you may be directed to sit and wait. Sit upright and don't slump. Refrain from looking at your phone. Instead, spend the time grounding yourself and feeling comfortable in the environment.
3. **When being directed into the interview room**, make eye contact and follow social cues as to whether or not to shake hands.
4. **If directed to stand**, position the feet in an 11 and 1 o'clock position to avoid swaying.
5. **If instructed to sit**, gently touch the top of the chair first before sitting to establish ownership and familiarity with your surroundings.
6. **During the meeting**, keep your hands forward and open so they can gesture easily. Place one foot slightly forward to direct your energy to the interviewer.
7. **During the meeting**, your shoulders will adjust to three different positions. In the beginning, your shoulders are typically forward in a "presenting" position that helps you engage the other person and emphasize more important information. As the meeting progresses, you may shift into a more "listen and

respond" angled sitting position. When the meeting wraps up, you may lean back in a relaxed "comfortable" position as you come to an understanding.

8. **Throughout the meeting**, eye contact is important. Of course, as you recall something or visualize something for the future you might look up to the right or left.
9. **When leaving the interview**, stand up, smile, and follow the person's lead by either nodding, shaking hands, or waving.
10. **Follow up** with an email or card that states your appreciation, recalls a specific moment in the interview that was memorable or insightful, and the benefits you can provide the team.

CHAPTER 10

TV or Social Media Hosting and Guesting

Over the years, I've coached numerous television and social media hosts and guests. One such talent is Berlin Fisher. Initially, I coached him on his guest presentation style as a beauty and style expert. Later, he needed a role adjustment when he became a segment host and correspondent covering a variety of genres and subjects. I included Fisher's interview here to share firsthand experience between those two roles: guest and host. It's the difference between going to the camera and letting the camera come to you. That change impacts how one stands, moves, listens, and responds. As you read this section, pay close attention to minor adjustments that impacted the outcome that you may want to "borrow."

BERLIN FISHER

California Live **TV host for NBC Bay Area**

> Elaine Clark gave me really great skills on how to move my body, speak differently, even edit what I said. When you're a guest, you want to say a lot. You're about trying to get as much information out as fast as you can. When you're a guest, you want to make a big splash. It's like, "Look at me—I'm the guest, pay attention." But when you're the host, you're the supporting actor, the "bus driver" making sure the segment flows. In that position, you have to learn how to pull back.
>
> One of the biggest things that I remember taking away from our "host" coaching sessions was that I was always stepping forward into the camera and pushing the information forward, like I did when I was a guest. Elaine taught me to bend my knee, lean back on my back

foot, and bring the audience in to me, what I was talking about, and what my guest was sharing. This was a big job shift to actually lay back, let the guest speak, and draw people in.

Another huge learning experience for me with Elaine was changing my language to be more inclusive and natural. Rather than say, "We're going to cook this particular item" or, "Can you show me and the guests at home how to do that?" Elaine taught me to use my hands and my body language to guide the action and say, "Can you show us how you made that?" Using the word "us" included me, the audience, and everybody. So, I didn't need to be so explanatory. I could bring people in casually and naturally to gain their interest and attention.

Another thing that I took away from our coaching sessions was to listen because the guest will give information that informs the next questions. I was always going, running through everything, and planning my moves. Elaine taught me to know my subjects and know what I was doing, but don't rehearse it because then it's not authentic. The host's job is to listen, respond, and guide the conversation.

One of the things I always hear about my segments on *California Life* is my authenticity. And that's because I don't rehearse it like I used to. Elaine taught me to become friends with my guests. Having been in that position before, I know what it's like to show up and the host is in the corner going over scripts, on their phone or whatever, and not connecting with me. Elaine taught me to become friends with my guests because that translates on-air. Ask friendly questions: Are you married? Do you have children? What do you do besides this? What are your hobbies? Then, when we're on TV and I'm in an interview and see that the guest is struggling I've got something that I can pull from and say: Tell us how this affects you and your family. Do your kids like to do this? Are you able to do this when you're skateboarding?

Years later, these tips are still working for me a hundred percent. I get a lot of accolades for my hosting abilities. I invested my first paycheck in coaching with Elaine and got tenfold back. You have to invest in yourself if you want to move forward.

MEDIA PREP AND PERFORMANCE

Here are some steps to follow to help you feel confident before, during, and after the TV or social media guest or host event.

1. **Prepare Your Mind**: Distill what you want to say into simple thoughts and words. If you know what you're talking about, you'll know what to say.
2. **Know Your Job**: Do you need to guide the conversation or listen and respond?
3. **Choose Your Attitude**: Based on the subject matter, decide how you want to connect with the audience and other people on the show. Do you want to educate, inform, surprise, excite, challenge, explore . . . ?
4. **Prepare Your Body**: Let the attitude dictate your movements and feelings. If you're feeling nervous, shake it out, loosen up, and relax the muscles.
5. **Position Your Hands**: If you're standing, keep your hands and gestures at waist level.
6. **Begin and End Strong**: Start with a simple movement that draws focus. At the end, allow your feelings about the subject matter show.

INTERVIEW TECHNIQUES—YOU GOT THIS!

Back on Track—It's easy to get derailed by an off-topic question or comment. Come up with a few comments that are unique to you and that you feel comfortable using that put your message back on track.

- "I wasn't expecting that! Let's pick up where we left off."
- "Remind me to get to that at the end if we still have time."
- "Before we get off topic, let's finish this . . . "

Recap—At the end, wrap it up with a brief summary of the top one to three takeaways.

Loose Lips Sink Ships—Nothing is ever off the record. It's easy to slip up and say something you don't want repeated. Even if it's not recorded or written down, it can easily be regurgitated later.

Remember the Audience—Questions, comments, and answers should be suitable to the outlet and final audience. Keep statements short for broadcast and mainstream media. Longer formats can accommodate lengthier and more elaborate conversations.

Be Yourself—Use personal anecdotes to illustrate your points. Make the interviewer see you as a person and not just a business representative or corporate stooge. Kick off the interview by asking *them* a personal question.

Make Yourself Relatable—The more audiences like you, the more they will pay attention to your message.

Be Genuine—Don't be afraid to be yourself. Imbue the information with your personal stamp.

Don't Repeat Negatives—Avoid being negative. If you have to say something negative, say it faster than the positive information so you toss it off and "throw it away."

Take the High Road—Rather than diss the competition, spin a positive response like "They do great work. Today we're here to talk about [fill in the blank with your key message phrase]."

Spin Oops! into Okay—Be truthful. Honest mistakes can be tolerated. There is nothing wrong with saying, "Oops, I made a mistake. Let me correct that statistic/number/statement."

CHAPTER 11

Sales

Companies tend to have their own vocabulary and product titles. It's often assumed that the recipient knows that internal information. It's always a good idea to do research on the company and people you're talking to, so the sales message isn't rote and generic, but rather it's custom tailored to their needs. Often time pressures—like thirty-minute Zoom meetings—mean each minute is filled with nonstop information. Instead, allow time to listen to the customer.

Never say, "Like I said . . ." Instead, slow down, rephrase the answer, and explain it a different way. Listening is your friend! Remember that *how* the client benefits from the product is way more important than *what* the product is.

Sometimes knowing too much can veer an interview off course. That is especially true with people who have a long, involved history at the company. Rather than speaking about the direct benefits of a product or service, the message can sink deep into the minutia mud of how it works. With all this internal information swarming in the head—be it the founder, executive, sales team, or other company employee—the one-word need must be defined. This single focus adds clarity for the speaker as well as the audience. It allows them to understand the concept and know what to do with the information. This leads to intentions and intended outcomes: to invest, to purchase, to explore, to suggest, to research, to accept, to appreciate, etc.

In this interview, Mylene Yao shares her experience defining and simplifying her message and how it helped her stay on point and enabled her sales team to become more efficient and effective speakers, too.

MYLENE YAO, M.D.

Co-founder and CEO, UNIVFY® Inc.

When I first started the company, I realized I needed to communicate what we do with different stakeholders. I had to pitch investors and do media interviews. I had these long sentences written out because I was more used to communicating in academic discussions with physicians and scientists or writing grant applications, scientific papers, and things of that nature. I realized I didn't know how to make the sentences shorter, more direct, and easier to understand.

In my first few sessions with Elaine, I realized she has this amazing ability to mentally capture all the information I was saying as I was speaking. When I paused, in real time she would edit verbally back to me how I should say something to make it easier to understand. She did this without writing notes, looking at my script, or anything. She would go boom, boom, boom, boom, boom. And I was like, wow! Can I record that? Because she just took my very long and windy scripts that I spoke and turned it into something very easy to digest, that was very punchy and perfect.

So now I just needed to learn, "How does she do that?" Elaine would give me examples and techniques. At first, I tried to copy her examples, write everything down, and then gradually realized that I need more coaching to feel more comfortable and have a greater ability to effectively communicate.

I also worked with Elaine to take some of her bullet-point style into our collateral materials so it would be direct and easy to understand. Everyone has a zillion things on their minds. If you can make printed and spoken information easier to understand, it helps everybody.

Running a startup technology company, I didn't have a marketing and sales background. The concepts and approaches I learned from Elaine really helped me work with my PR, marketing, and sales teams. I brought her in for team and individual coaching so they could work together on general concepts and individually for specific adaptations and adjustments. Taking complicated materials and distilling the information into more powerful communication—both internally among the team and externally to our clients and vendors—is always good if you can understand one another better.

CHAPTER 12
Legal

Attorneys need to be confident, persuasive, clear, concise, and organized. They need the ability to evaluate facts, identify legal issues, assess risks, and think critically and strategically, while advocating for their clients, upholding the rule of law, and positively contributing to the legal profession. That's a lot of balls to juggle! The mind has a big job of applying legal principles to solve complex problems creatively and effectively. And let's not forget how the body, voice, movements, gestures, and word emphasis support the legal arguments.

The following are three different legal applications and styles with corresponding informational interviews. This first one, with Peter Borruso, demonstrates how a law student sought help outside the confines of law school curriculum to improve his use of body language and words to appear more confident and persuasive. Those same physical and auditory adjustments now serve him in court trials before a jury and judge.

PETER BORRUSO

Deputy Public Defender; Trial Attorney at Law

> When I was in law school, I knew becoming a trial attorney was the ultimate goal. The problem was, I knew nothing about how to present myself persuasively and confidently in front of an audience. I turned to the only person I knew who could help me with this dilemma . . . Elaine Clark. She taught me that every single nuance in my body language, enunciation of each word, and force of my words would need to be perfected for me to become what I am today, a trial attorney who has completed over fifty jury trials. The foundation of what I learned still resonates with me today in each closing argument I make.

MOCK TRIAL

Many high schools, colleges, and universities have mock trial teams and clubs. A mock trial competition is an educational activity where participants enact a criminal case in a courtroom setting, arguing constitutional issues before real judges and attorneys. Students plan, draft, and present opening statements, direct examinations, cross-examinations, and closing arguments. Courtroom roles include attorney, witness, defendant, clerk, bailiff, and timekeeper. Mock trials are designed to teach students about the legal system, critical thinking, teamwork, persuasive communication, and public speaking.

If you haven't seen a mock trial, it is quite impressive! Judges who score the prosecution and defense teams often comment how they wish the attorneys in their courtroom were as polished and prepared as these students. Of course, the team spends all or part of the school year preparing one case, a luxury that few attorneys can afford. Here's how it works.

Preparation

Case Materials: Teams are given a fictional case (civil or criminal) in advance. The case packet includes the case summary, witness statements, evidence, exhibits, relevant laws, and legal precents.

Team Roles: Teams prepare both prosecution/plaintiff and defense arguments, as they will perform both sides in different rounds.

- Attorneys prepare opening/closing statements, direct/cross-examinations, and legal arguments.
- Witnesses memorize their statements and practice their roles to portray characters credibly.
- Timekeepers monitor time during trial proceedings.

Trial Rounds

Mock trials take place in real or simulated courtrooms with a real or volunteer judge and sometimes a jury.

The trial consists of three primary sections:

1. **Opening Statements**, where each side presents a preview of their case to the judge/jury.

2. **Witness Testimony**, where attorneys call witnesses to the stand for:
   - Direct examination: Friendly questioning to build the case.
   - Cross-examination: Opposing attorneys challenge the witness's credibility or testimony.
3. **Closing Arguments**, where each side summarizes their case, highlights key points of evidence, and argues for a favorable verdict.

Scoring

Judges (often real attorneys, judges, or educators) evaluate teams on the following:

- Quality of arguments and legal reasoning
- Public speaking and presentation skills
- Adherence to trial procedure and rules of evidence
- Realistic portrayal of witnesses and professionalism

The verdict (guilty/not guilty or liable/not liable) may not affect the scoring. Instead, points are awarded based on performance.

Advancing in Competition

Teams compete in multiple rounds. High-scoring teams advance to finals, and winners are often recognized individually (e.g., Best Attorney, Best Witness) and as a team.

Attorney coaches and mock trial coaches guide their teams to collaborate and build logical thinking and writing skills. As the speech, movement, and performance coach I helped them develop their characters, walk and talk with confidence, create a presence that captures attention, controls the room, and holds their ground like a "winner." Together we placed in and won numerous county, state, and national Empire competitions.

I can't say enough good things about the benefits of participating in a high school or college mock trial team. As far as I'm concerned, it's the full speaker immersion training package: public speaking, critical thinking, acting, and teamwork. Each member needs to write and perform using the power of persuasion; stand, walk, and gesture confidently; be aware of timing and pacing constraints; decide on an effective tone and attitude; have a clear motivation, intentions, need, and emotions; speak so others can hear the message clearly; and embrace spontaneity and change directions as needed.

When I first started working with Philip Wilder and his team, the students were resistant. In their minds, their collective brain power, analyses, and thought processes were enough. But that's *not* enough. Speaking to achieve a winning result is about incorporating the whole body . . . not just the brain. Before long, the students understood that using every tool in the body-mind toolkit is needed to perform at the highest standards.

PHILIP WILDER

Teacher and Mock Trial Coach, Moreau Catholic High School

> I'll try and give you an opening statement as to why I think you would benefit from the speech and movement coaching that Elaine Clark provided to us and the team. It's not just words but the ways in which we speak that are effective. To watch the transformation that took place was truly remarkable. The mind is like a parachute when it's open. She would give great critiques and the students began to learn a lot of the tools, would help each other, and pass things along. That helped the kids in the hardest competitions.
>
> We called our team the Honey Badgers because they're famous for their strength, ferocity, and toughness. Some students in the mock trial club went on to become attorneys. Whether students went into law didn't matter. It's about life skills, speaking critically and with confidence. How to hold the body, walk on thinking lines and stop when delivering the key message, using the hands, intonation, asking a question, the power of the . . . pause. If you don't have that in your toolbox, we're not as effective speakers as we "think" we are.

As Martin Camp describes in the next interview, public speaking is frightening to many people. Attorneys need to be confident and competent word merchants, even if they're in the early years of learning how to become one. While the job description has serious consequences, humor, laughter, and storytelling support advocacy. Trust is also a major factor, not just at a speaking event, but with client meetings and in the courtroom.

MARTIN L. CAMP

Assistant Dean for Graduate and International Programs; Professor of Practice, SMU Dedman School of Law

During my time as Faculty in Residence at Crum Commons, Southern Methodist University, we were most fortunate to have Elaine Clark talk to the students at one of our weekly Traditions. I have to admit, it was one of the best attended and most helpful of the presentations they received that school year. Elaine exudes both empathy and confidence. Public speaking is very frightening to most people and my freshmen and sophomores that night was no exception. Elaine's coaching was impactful and also humorous. Getting people to laugh is one way to reduce stress. She immediately connected with the audience. She is a natural coach, mentor, and storyteller. The practical exercises she took the students through that night I know they will remember and use throughout their studies and careers.

Elaine spoke to my law school class about the power of your voice and its use in advocacy. I always tell my students that "Confidence comes from Competence and Competence comes from Experience." Elaine reinforced this message and mantra. She helped the students understand the importance of "finding your voice," "using your voice as a communication tool," and understanding the audience who will be hearing your voice. These are all very important skills for lawyers who are "word merchants." Whether speaking to a judge, at an administrative hearing, to a jury, or negotiating with the opposing counsel, preparing by thinking of these three skills she discussed allows lawyers to reach their maximum communication and advocacy potential. I know my students gained more experience in her presentation that increased their competence and therefore confidence.

CHAPTER 13
Religion

Over the years, I've offered coaching and advice to an assortment of ministers, priests, and clergy. The common thread is that they sought additional guidance in how to improve one or all of the services they were called to do: sermons, ministry, and counseling. Within each congregation, there are also laypeople and volunteers who support their religious affiliation through scripture readings, announcements, committee involvement, and outreach. For those of you who wish to improve how you deliver your message in a faithful and trusting manner, I offer insights from two people.

The first is Denis Eucalyptus who is truly a Lazarus figure, having survived both being buried for hours in an avalanche and a dim prognosis for cancer. People of faith are not immune from challenging situations that seem insurmountable. During those moments, individuals and congregations expect uplift and support that a faith leader "called to serve" may not inherently have the full skills to provide. Supportive and organizational abilities that come from the heart and mind can be taught, but they're not always provided in "real time/real life" ways during the immersive sanctified learning process. That's why I asked Denis to share his experience of "finding his voice" behind the pulpit, in meetings, and in personal counseling, so others are aware of expectations and adaptations that are required of clergy. A reader facing the same challenges, as a giver or receiver, can likewise make adjustments accordingly.

DENIS EUCALYPTUS

Retired Minister

Here are some of Denis's insights about sermons, ministry, and counseling.

Sermons

When I was at seminary, there was only a one-semester class on preaching. It didn't go into the nuts and bolts of putting together a sermon or the different styles of preaching. It was more generic, listening to some good sermons with a few people getting a chance to preach. During my first couple years in the ministry, I became aware that I was a pretty poor preacher. I was trying to be a manuscript preacher and it sounded like I was writing a paper for seminary rather than speaking from the heart to my congregation. So, I took a three-week intensive class to learn a new style.

At first, I was fearful of putting aside the manuscript and to preach with just a half-page of notes. After a bit of practice, that basic outline kept me from wandering off so I could use my precious twenty minutes to preach the sermon. It also allowed me to step away from the pulpit and walk down a couple steps so the people could see me, and I could speak to the congregation in an authentic way.

Preaching is not a lecture. It's communicating something of the heart. Saying something about what you really trust and why you trust it. We're talking about trusting God, trusting the spirit, trusting the goodness of the universe . . . or whatever. FAITH = TRUST.

That should move you to the focus of the sermon:

- Social justice
- Holy Day celebrations
- Storytelling
- Move a person to have more love in their life
- Reach out and touch other people's lives
- Build friendships
- Be part of a community

People want to be moved by a sermon and not lectured to.

Ministry

In committee meetings and other situations, the first thing a pastor should do is listen. Hear where people are coming from first, then ask questions. The pastor should be clear and calm and open to a give and take. It's easy to get drawn into a fight and get defensive. The primary calling is to be a healer, accept, love, and not win battles. I was told that the minister's job is to come up with a hundred great ideas and maybe two or three or five of those ideas might take root each week. In other words, don't be too attached to the stuff, the plans, and how things should be. Be prepared to present what you're thinking and why, so you can get to the point and be able to compromise. Committees should be a workshop on how to be a community.

Counseling

When people are in the hospital, nursing home, dealing with a situation, or grieving, they don't need platitudes. There are no magical words. They want compassion and for their spiritual leader to just be there in a loving presence. They may want to hear a song that holds a deep remembrance and meaning that brings back some beloved times in that person's life. They may want a hug or their hand held. Or they may just want someone to sit in silence with them. Listening is the key to counseling so the response and actions fit their needs.

After this interview, I was reminded of the message of our family's pastor after my brother lost his fight with cancer. He said that in the old days, grief was made public to others by wearing a black dress or black armband. That symbol of grieving made people aware that, due to the loss, the person may not always act rationally and to allow them the courtesy of understanding.

I wish that visual symbol was still in common practice. Being unaware of what a person is going through can lead to communication faux pas. Along those lines, Parker Eng illustrates next how some people keep a running tally of verbal missteps. While it's never fun to have personal errors pointed out, awareness and perception can lead to practice and improvement.

PARKER ENG

Chairman of the Board, Probe Ministries

After someone in my church told me the number of ums and ahs he counted, I knew I needed coaching for our non-profit's Fiftieth Anniversary Banquet. I sent Elaine my speech before meeting on Zoom. She listened to me read it and quickly realized that many of the filler words and sounds I added were caused by long sentences, holding my body in one position, and gesturing the same way.

In just a few lessons, she helped me craft a powerful and engaging story, use shorter sentences to allow time to connect with the audience, build excitement for the event and the introduction of the other speakers, and convey the message with confidence. I was able to practice and implement each of the tips.

She empowered me to embrace my unique voice and style, use a variety of gestures, slow down and take in the moment, and make the experience enjoyable and memorable. I resonated with the audience from the moment I stepped on stage. Thanks to her expert coaching, I was able to deliver my speech in a way that had the audience excited and laughing, setting the perfect tone for the evening's celebration. Oh, and this time . . . no one counted any ums and ahs.

CHAPTER 14

News

I've had the pleasure of refining the presentation skills of numerous reporters, anchors, journalists, weather reporters, and traffic reporters in the greater Northern California Bay Area. Every news contributor must demonstrate experience with how they report and interview that goes beyond conveying knowledge of the media business and their assigned subject matter. Nuance, style, personality, and perspective play a huge role in gaining audience trust and relatability. A signature slogan may be needed to start or end a program while other journalists may rely more on a specific movement, camera angle, or attitude to set them apart. In all cases, the news person has been invited into someone's home or onto a device they're holding in their hand. The camera should be treated like the eyes of a friend that viewers feel they know.

NEWS ANCHOR

The news anchor is the face of the news program, delivering stories from the studio, and tying the different segments together while standing or sitting behind a desk. In many studios, the reporter has to shift focus when the red light changes from one camera teleprompter to another. This change is often used to segue from an intense topic to a feel-good piece. Abrupt emotional shifts require that the anchor shift gears quickly to adapt to the urgency or empathy. They may do this by looking down then up in a different direction, shuffling papers on the desk, picking up or putting down a pen, gesturing with the opposite hand, and so forth.

Add to that the complexity of listening and talking while getting updates in their earpiece from the control room, time constraints of each segment as it wraps around the tosses to reporters and special guests plus advertising breaks, and the comradery and banter with their co-host and others in the studio who report weather, traffic, and sports.

Sitting at the news desk, it looks best when the anchor sits upright, has one or both hands on the desk, and has one or both elbows out so the body appears confident and well defined.

REPORTER

There are several types of reporters who are hired on their experience, background, and program requirements. Producers oversee the show's content, assign stories, and coordinate with reporters. The camera crew work with field reporters to capture footage and live shots. Editors compile and refine the video segments for broadcast. Assignment editors manage the story leads and reporter assignments.

- **Field**—Correspondents who provide on-the-scene coverage of live or pre-recorded events, conduct interviews with eyewitnesses or officials, gather and deliver real-time updates.
- **Investigative**—In-depth reporting of complex issues and long-form stories that often takes weeks or months of preparation to uncover facts through extensive research and interviews.
- **Weather Reporters and Meteorologists**—Utilizing specialized graphics and meteorological data to explain weather patterns, they deliver daily and extended forecasts, and provide updates during severe weather conditions.
- **Sports**—Local, national, and international reporting of scores, highlights, and player statistics in sports-related stories, post-game interviews, and live events.
- **Traffic**—Monitor the road conditions; report live on delays, closures, and accidents; and advise viewers on alternate routes or transit options.
- **Entertainment**—Focuses on pop culture, movies, TV, music, and celebrity news, reviews, and upcoming releases. They may also interview and report live at red carpet events.
- **Political**—Specializes in covering political news, campaigns, and government affairs; conducts interviews with politicians and analysts; and reports on legislative developments, elections, and political controversies.
- **Business and Economic**—Financial markets, corporate news, and complex economic trends and data are analyzed and broken down for the viewers to better understand what's going on in the stock market and how that relates to consumer issues and business developments.
- **Health**—Cover tips and resources for wellness and safety, discuss advancements in medicine, disease outbreaks, and healthcare policies, trends, news, and public health issues.
- **Technology**—Focus on technological advancements and digital trends including tech launches, cybersecurity issues, industry developments, review gadgets and discuss their implications.

- **Feature**—Delivering stories that aim to inspire or entertain such as human-interest stories, community events, unique profiles, lifestyle trends, and lighter, feel-good news.

Balancing out the news team so each reporter is unique and engaging is based on each individual's knowledge, experience, personality, voice, appearance, and style. Depending on the immediacy of the reporting, they should be up-to-date on supportive information, able to easily retain new information and data, and report directly to the camera, preferably without having to look at their notes.

Viewers are sensitive to traffic reporters who are not familiar with the roads or common pronunciations of the cities, as they demonstrate that they are not local to the area. To remedy that, they need to drive on the major roads and highways, visit cities to get a feel for them, and become "one with the market."

As weather reporting has advanced from green-screen still images the meteorologist points toward 3D images that they walk on or near, meteorologists need to practice on-set to get used to the location of virtual maps and objects and how the interaction appears on camera. For the other reporters, they need to match the attitude and perceived authority of the area of the business they're talking about. That can range from fun and playful for entertainment and sports, to knowledgeable and casually confident for financial reports, to concerned and serious for hard-edged news.

PANELS

When on a panel, listening is just as important as speaking. A moderator that knows and respects each panelist's primary expertise and knowledge base can guide the discussion, examine or argue a topic, and explore solutions. This informal debate style encourages and supports different points of view. Rather than having a lovefest of like-minded people agreeing with one another, most audiences want to hear varying viewpoints, so they get a more rounded perspective and make insightful decisions on their own.

Moderator Tips:

- Keep the intros and background information short.
- Begin with a question that is controversial or has inherently different points of view.
- Acknowledge who wants to speak and call on one person at a time.
- Don't let one or two people hijack the panel.
- Keep the discussion on track by calling on new panelists to add their insights.
- Be prepared to rephrase the question, add additional information that connects or clarifies perspectives, or inform panelists that you're moving on to the next topic.
- If a topic takes off, keep it going and let the audience know why it's important.
- Don't let the topic or panelists' contributions fizzle out.
- Acknowledge when it's time to move on.
- Close with a takeaway statement that defines the experience.

Panelist Tips:

- Confidently share a unique perspective and experience.
- Be clear, concise, and avoid lengthy monologues.
- Actively listen to, respond, and build upon contributions by the moderator and other panelists.
- Acknowledge and value different perspectives.
- Offer counterpoints and ask questions.

MULTIMEDIA JOURNALIST

A multimedia journalist often works alone. They get the assignment, drive to the location, set up their own camera, perform interviews, and shoot supporting visuals. Then (sometimes in their car or the back of a tricked-out work van), they edit the video, write the script package, record the voice-over, and upload the segment through a digital delivery system, and drive home.

Developing a personal style depends on the types of assignments a multimedia journalist is assigned. It may be environmental, tech, investigative, opinion, breaking news, business, or as one of my coaching clients called two reporting types . . . the critter beat (animals) and the puddle report (weather). Framing the camera so it shows an interaction with the location may mean talking while squatting down to feel the dirt before standing up, walking two or three steps toward the camera, or interviewing someone with the discussed location clearly in the background.

When watching the news, most people don't spend a lot of time thinking about the research, structure, storyline, framing, verbiage, timing, or tone of the piece. Based on the studio assignment, journalists make that decision and try their best to deliver the message effectively within the allotted time frame. A narrative piece may take a few days, a daily news report may take a few hours, and breaking news can be instantaneous. In addition to being knowledgeable of the subject matter and people involved, journalists need to be adaptive and think on their feet as they glean the best visual and auditory information that can relay a cohesive and informative story. Wilson Walker provides an insight into this fast-paced journalistic journey and how the voice plays an integral part in it.

WILSON WALKER

Reporter, CBS News Bay Area

When I'm doing a story, I generally don't think primarily about what I'm going to say. Everything I say is there to connect what is left unsaid, like the who, what, when, and where. I think of it more as the connective tissue.

My preference is to start the stories with some sound and feel like I'm there to report what's happening. How heavy do we have to be? Can we joke about that? I figure that out, so it speaks to a kind of mood and vibe.

Stories that I do that I think are good are the stories that don't necessarily have the best video or the best sound. It's where everything comes together, and the story has the right feel. For example, when I'm putting a story out there about a fire, someone is usually going to say, "I tell you, the fire just came out of nowhere. It came over the hill. The next thing I knew, we had to run."

That sets the stage. It's the perfect way to start. Correspondingly, someone will generally say something to the effect of, "I just can't believe it all happened. I don't know where we're going to go from here."

That's a nice way to end the story. So now I have the beginning and the end already and I don't have to write or say anything. In the middle, I add the other six or seven sound bites. After it's edited, I write little pieces that hold the rest of it together.

If it's a really slow methodical thing about AI and whether AI takes our jobs, which is not exciting television visually speaking anyway, you know I'm still starting with the interview with the CEO and the professor at Berkeley. But how do we take that and make a story out of that? I can't make that up, right? And so, I'm thinking of all these ingredients that have to come together. What I actually say is the last thing I do.

There's an infinite spectrum of different kind of stories. And I think good stories for me often are like, "That story had the right touch." You know it's serious but how serious? Sometimes things are kind of serious, but not so serious, and it's like figuring out what the degree of seriousness is and not faking it. When I worked with you, Elaine, we go to the idea of a voice, right in the voice-over. You can have a good idea of what it should sound like. But it's a little harder to make it happen. It doesn't just pop out of your mouth, right? You have to concentrate a little bit, and I like getting it there.

CHAPTER 15
Sports

Live stadium public address (PA) announcing has its own set of challenges. The PA announcer has to know the rules of the game, when to talk and for how long, and the names and numbers of the home team and visiting players; keep the fans engaged and excited from the minute they enter the stadium to well after the game is over; stay focused and not be distracted by the stadium slap-back, delay, and echo; relay stats and history; write scripts; read scripts; announce events and sponsorships; record commercials; attend PR events; engage their social media audience; and represent the team at various functions. Preparation for each game starts hours before the announcer begins speaking to the crowds.

I've provided team coaching at CBS Sports, various individual TV reporting at Pac-12 sporting events, and to the baseball stadium announcer for the Oakland A's. I was contracted to work pre-season and opening games with Amelia Schimmel to control her voice, calm her nerves, and lean into her knowledge and passion for baseball as she journeyed from announcing during the COVID pandemic to an empty stadium dotted with cutout characters in seats to fans returning in person to cheer on their team.

If you're interested in sports announcing, prepare yourself for hours of pre-game research and sudden changes; staying up-to-date on the latest game rules; properly pronouncing player names with finesse and gusto; reading commercials and sponsorship information live or in a pre-event recording session; energizing the audience; using the voice and message to direct focus to the field or other locations; working in tandem with the video monitor, graphics, and stats people; ad-libbing fun or insightful comments; adjusting to the PA audio delay and sound bounce; keeping the game moving; and directing the crowd to safely exit the stadium. With Amelia Schimmel, other duties include tasting the snacks fans send her and posting comments about them on social media!

Another thing that is not often talked about is knowing how much to eat or drink prior to a game when the opportunity to take a break may not happen for over three hours. (Yikes!) There's also the tricky act of pressing a button to speak and releasing the button when finished so unintended information doesn't get projected to a crowd of thousands. But most of all, sports announcers need to *love* the game! Schimmel, a super fan, definitely fits that description.

AMELIA SCHIMMEL

PA announcer for the Athletics (baseball), SJ Barracudas (ice hockey), Bay FC (soccer) and fill in for other sports including swim meets, lacrosse, water polo, soccer, softball, gymnastics, and the San Jose Sharks.

PA announcing takes place in the controlled chaos of the control room, where everyone's on computers controlling a different piece of the video board. It's in stark contrast to the press box where everyone is quietly watching the game and taking notes. I start out with an opening greeting. Mine is "It's a beautiful day for baseball," because even if it's rainy, windy, or smoky, it's always a beautiful day for baseball.

And then I introduce myself: "I'm Amelia Schimmel, welcoming you to the Oakland Coliseum, Ricky Henderson Field. This is game one of a three-game set between the visiting Texas Rangers and the Athletics." Then I announce different nonprofit and community sponsorships, so they understand what the nonprofit does and why we're hyping up a company that's giving donations or fan prizes. We play my pre-recorded safety, evacuation, don't curse, be civil, no fighting voice-over and video. We work in the ceremonial information and get ready for those people to do their thing. Then, the producer coordinates with the team to stop warming up and be ready to stand for the national anthem. The team runs out and I introduce each player and what number they're wearing. And then I call the first pitch.

Behind the scenes I'm writing scripts and checking stats. Inning by inning I'm announcing batters and in-game features. During the inning breaks that are about two minutes, I do some kind of sponsorship element. Fans send me unique local snacks that I taste before the game and post a quick review and rating of zero-to-ten on social media as my #snackofthegame. When it's an exceptional game, I wait for the hugs, high fives, and moment to play out, then let everyone know what just happened and why they're celebrating because there are some fans that are not necessarily deep into the baseball world, and they need to know. Then I do my walkout, drive home safely stuff. And, of course, I have a button to push when I speak and take my finger off when I'm done, so my voice only goes out into the stadium at the appropriate times. That's not to say that there are not some occasional malfunctions.

Before a larger crowd of real fans started filtering back in, the A's front office told me it was time to get some proper training. I was thrilled because I thought that I was doing things that weren't going to help sustain my voice. I was talking too loudly or going too fast. And had no real understanding of how to create good inflection in my voice and vary my reads enough to really sound professional and polished. And that's why they sent me to Elaine.

In just a few sessions, I felt better, was less nervous, and more polished. I didn't realize that sometimes just the things you write and the symbols you scribble in the script—like an arrow up or down—was something I could do beforehand. There are a number of things we worked on, like opening up my chest and pushing the energy down through my body rather than entirely through my mouth.

I'm in a control room with many people, and I didn't think that gesturing was something that I should be doing and was a little embarrassed by it even. And then I realized I shouldn't worry what anybody else in the room thinks because the majority of people in the stadium, 40,000 sometimes, are hearing my voice. And if it makes my voice sound better, it really doesn't matter what my body is doing as long as it's comfortable for me. When something was tall, I got really big and really tall, if something was round, I would gesture in motions that were rounded.

I had a lot of nervousness and tension that I was holding in my throat and I would sometimes stutter through reads. So, Elaine had me pushing my hand onto the desk or pushing my energy through my feet and into the floor. Realizing that I can use the rest of my body was hugely helpful. I use these techniques and others she taught me when I announce and emcee other sports and charity events.

CHAPTER 16

Social Media Influencers

Providing visual and audio-based content for social media platforms is immediate and interactive. Influencers rely heavily on their personality, relatability, and connection with their followers. They build influence through direct engagement, comments, likes, and live streams. Some people aspire to be influencers as their business goal while others are approached by companies to create content in exchange for financial compensation or free product.

If you're an influencer or plan to be one, here are four main components of your performance that you should consider when sharing with your audience.

1. Lean into your unique personality and look so that it stands out and differentiates you from other influencers in this crowded space. If you're unsure what makes you unique, refer back to the strengths and weaknesses list you created.
2. Be confident in yourself, your content, and your opinions. Even if you mess up, own the mistake, and share how others can learn from this human and unplanned moment.
3. Add your authentic humor, wit, or charm to enhance your audience appeal and foster loyalty.
4. Explore camera angles, framing, lighting, sound, product placement, and actions that encourage people to stop scrolling, turn up the sound, and watch for twenty seconds or more.

While influencer content is short, that doesn't mean it doesn't take thought, planning, and time to execute, edit, post, and follow up. This can be through clickable links, live chats, comments, prizes and challenges, bonus materials, direct messages, references, and other forms of audience involvement.

This next interview is with Anne Ganguzza, a voice actor, coach, host, producer, and presenter. I was Anne's first interviewee as a trailblazing pioneer in the voice-over industry on her podcast #VO B.O.S.S. Ganguzza uses her business and voice-over skills as a visual media influencer to shape, create, and demonstrate products, gear, and fashion.

ANNE GANGUZZA

Fashion and Studio Gear Influencer, Anne Ganguzza Voice Productions

> The skills I developed through voice-over and podcasting have been instrumental in my transition to influencer on-camera work. While my career began with engaging audiences using only my voice, podcasting provided a unique platform to refine my conversational style, fostering trust and connection week after week. These experiences taught me that authenticity begins with preparation—knowing your message, believing in it, and delivering it as naturally as possible. Translating this to on-camera work required embracing physical expressiveness and authenticity as well, while staying true to my voice. It is helpful to practice aligning your words, tone, and body language so they reinforce one cohesive message, making your delivery more impactful and relatable.
>
> Now, as I evolve into an on-camera presence, I draw upon nearly two decades of experience in storytelling and connection. My goal is to merge the authenticity of my voice with the visual elements of on-camera communication, creating a relatable and engaging presence that resonates with audiences and empowers brands to connect more deeply. To be successful, it's absolutely essential to embrace vulnerability and share your story in a way that feels real and unscripted. I have learned over and over that it is not about perfection; it's about being approachable and human. By focusing on building trust and staying consistent with your message across platforms, you can create meaningful connections that inspire and captivate your audience.

CHAPTER 17

Voice-Overs

There are many applications for using one's voice for fun and profit. The various areas of the industry include radio and TV commercials, online ads and social media, e-learning and education videos, explainer videos, animation and cartoons, video games, anime, dubbing and ADR looping, corporate training videos, promotional videos, telephone and IVR systems, event announcements, movie trailers, news and radio broadcasting, audiobooks, documentaries, in-show narration, audio description for blind audiences, and off-stage announcements at live events, award shows, and conventions. Each voice-over performance style has its own set of skills, challenges, and expectations.

If you want to explore this business further, you'll find detailed information in my book *There's Money Where Your Mouth Is: A Complete Insider's Guide to Earning Income and Building a Career in Voice-Overs*. For the purposes of this book, we'll concentrate on two areas of the business where authors and documentary filmmakers often seek coaching and guidance.

AUDIOBOOK

While some authors may choose to use an AI-synthesized voice to record their book, they should take note that the heart and soul of the message will be missing. The tone, pitch, and cadence of the words will go up and down and sound pretty, but the artificial voice will not bring history, opinion, natural intonation, and emotional depth to the story. Only a human can do that.

When an author, celebrity, or voice actor records an audiobook, they provide the narrative thread and "voice" of the author. Therefore, it's important to understand the genre and subject matter, style of the book, why the book was written, and how they can relate that storytelling skill to the listener. Voicing the dialogue of the people and characters should support the story narrative, tone, and message. Subtle and effective changes to the voice can be created by changing vocal pitch, rhythm, voice texture, attitude, emotion, personality, background, age, and gender. When choosing a voice, keep the listener's comfort and your vocal health in mind so the voice performance encourages imagination without being jarring or overly dramatic to the listener. Overly dramatic voice performances can potentially fatigue and stress the narrator's voice. The narrative voice of the book should paint a picture in the listener's imagination. If character voices are needed, their distinct personalities and perspectives should support and enrich the overall story. For specific information about key deliverable requirements and opportunities for audiobook narrators, visit www.findawayvoices.com by Spotify and www.acx.com for Audible.

DOCUMENTARY

There are amazing documentary narrators that combine technical skills, emotional intelligence, and the ability to bring a script to life in a way that resonates with the audience and enhances the storytelling. The voice maintains a stable and professional tone throughout that supports the picture rather than drawing focus on oneself. The style of speaking can be a first-person perspective, a third-person narrative, or a dynamic delivery that adjusts voice modulation to emphasize key points or transitions. There may be reenactments of historical characters that need to match that time period and manner of speech.

Most documentary filmmakers spend years bringing their vision to life. When it comes to narrating their own film, some realize that they need an outside perspective and coaching. Adjusting the purpose, placement, tone, and pacing of a filmmaker's narration is an area I particularly enjoy. A story arc needs to be established that begins with the attention-grabbing opening, employs various tempos and attitudes in the middle, and concludes with a feeling and understanding that resonates with the audience.

Defining that one-word "need" for the film that encapsulates the reason for sharing this story snaps the narration into place and gives it purpose. Movements and gestures that subtly support the action lend variety and interest to the words, retaining audience attention. Emotional changes throughout add empathy for the audience to also experience. And the authoritative tone is based on perspective, whether as part of the story or as an outside observer.

When these techniques are applied, the before-and-after versions of the voice narration are startling once the performance is dropped from the head to the heart.

CHAPTER 18
Gaming

Video game industry professionals use their voices in many ways. In addition to voice acting, casting, directing, producing, and audio engineering dozens of video games, I've coached teams and individual game hosts, reporters, panelists, and directors at several major game companies including Blizzard, GameSpot, CBS Interactive, and Electronic Arts.

During individual, full- or half-day group sessions, we address their particular needs and ways to achieve their anticipated outcomes. These include:

- Empowerment and confidence-building techniques.
- Being more relaxed and natural on camera and in virtual meetings.
- Engaging the audience and drawing them in.
- Defining the message to reach desired outcomes and goals.
- Voice, diction, pitch, and modulation improvement.
- Identifying personal challenges at the event and ways to address them.
- Building a toolkit of effective methods to use, practice, and improve.

Here are a few of the challenges that are specific to this industry.

PANELS AND "CONS"

While the list continues to grow, some popular gaming conventions include: Gamescom, PAX, E3, Comic-Con, GDC, TwitchCon, SXSW Gaming Expo, QuakeCon, Otakon, TGS, and BlizzCon. The convention floor, panels, and presentations are filled with prominent presenters, industry execs, game developers, designers, industry journalists, and fans of all sorts, including some attendees who are "larping," where they dress as particular characters and even act out their parts in the game.

With many stars and well-known panelists there to share their insights, the host has to plan a strategy for keeping the questions focused and the answers limited so everyone on the panel is allowed a relatively equal chance to speak in the limited time allowed. When hosting a panel, think about what the fans most want to know about each of the key players in the game.

AMBUSH JOURNALISM

Journalists at these busy events have to plan a tactic for who they want to interview and the primary questions they want answered. Fighting the crowds or positioning oneself in unexpected places to intercept a potentially uncooperative person requires dexterity, knowledge, research, and charm. When a microphone and camera are thrown in a person's face the journalist needs to quickly connect with the person and make them feel comfortable enough to share interesting insights that possibly no other reporter achieved.

Planning, practice, and role-playing prior to the conference can help define expectations and calm nerves.

CHAPTER 19

Disabilities and Additional Needs

Teachers, students, camp directors, and parents may want to pay particular attention to this section. Working with children to use specific kinesthetic movements in a fun improvisation, drama, and theatrical manner, fundamentally changed how I coach, teach, and perform. Movement encourages muscle memory and comprehension. I'm excited to share a few of these drama games and activities with you. To download the full Special Focus, Inc. program, go to ElaineClarkVO.com/special-focus.

Background: For ten years, my business partner Joe Schmitz and I were awarded a grant to create and implement a school drama program to support the personal growth of students with mild-to-moderate disabilities. We developed an interactive program that opens the door to students with diverse challenges such as autism, cognitive delay, emotional disabilities, attention deficit disorders, speech difficulties, diverse physical needs, and neurodiversity.

This fun and engaging program uses:

- Improvisation activities that instill a positive attitude while developing creativity, focus, and attention.
- Theatre arts and storytelling that develop narrative and communication skills while exploring emotions, relationships, and responses to life situations.
- A curriculum that supports literacy, reasoning, and physical development.
- Training teachers in the "Special Focus" approach so they can use it in their own teaching.

The program aligns with California Common Core State Standards for K-12:

- **English Language Arts**. Make a kinesthetic game out of identifying parts of speech and using them to build clear sentences. Play games that identify the 5 W's (who, what, why, when, where) and give presentations about the story.
- **Narrative**. Use performing arts to improvise a story with a clear narrative arc and identify relevant information that "moves the story forward." Act out characters to demonstrate different behaviors and qualities, consider how others perceive them, and develop vocabulary to describe them.
- **Science**. Make science concepts, such as electromagnetism and gravity, real by acting them out. Use games to check understanding and retention.
- **Research and Investigation**. Use mock interviews to develop investigation skills while reviewing subject matter.

Teacher perspectives:

- "This kinesthetic learning approach brings social studies to life. Students really get into it."
- "Integrating these improv activities into science lessons is the first time every student understood the subject."
- "Acting out stories really brought reading to life and improved comprehension and involvement."

DRAMA GAMES AND ACTIVITIES FOR SCHOOL, CAMP, AND HOME

Sound Ball

Summary

Students mime throwing an imaginary "ball of sound" to someone else, who mimes catching the ball and making the same sound. The student who caught the ball then throws a new sound ball to another student.

Skills developed

- Eye contact
- Sequencing, imagination, creativity, and abstract thinking
- Listening, verbalizing, repeating

Measures of success

- Participate, listen, and be attentive
- Make eye contact to demonstrate that they are ready
- Accept other's ideas and repeat the sound they are given
- Student is willing to participate
- Follow correct sequence of receiving and sending
- Perceive the characteristics of an imaginary object and react appropriately

Procedure

1. Students form a circle.
2. Teacher introduces the activity by saying something such as "We're going to play a game called Sound Ball. See this ball? It's an invisible ball of sound. And I can throw it to someone. Then they'll catch it with the sound I made. Like this . . ."
3. Starter throws an imaginary ball with an accompanying sound to another staff member who acts out catching the ball in a way that reflects the ball's weight and size, and the speed it was thrown.
4. The person who catches the ball throws a new sound ball to someone else.
5. **Note:** Each person makes two sounds: The first is the sound of the ball when they catch the ball. The second sound is a new sound that they pass to another student.
6. Continue until everyone has participated and the class seems ready to go to the next activity.
7. Complete game by having someone put the "ball" in their pocket.

Variations

- Throw emotional faces. Introduce the face by name the first time you throw it. For example, "I'm going to throw a happy face," then make a happy face and throw that. There's no need for other players to keep repeating the name of the face after it's introduced.
- Pass terms from other subject matter such as months, arithmetic, colors, or class rules.

Notes

- This typically requires several throws for students to understand the sequence.
- Encourage students to make their own unique sound when they throw the ball.
- Have students give positive invisible balls, or "a ball that you'd like to receive."
- For students who don't have a lot of expressive language, Sound Ball is a valuable way to start students communicating. It can bring out expressive communication in a child that doesn't have it naturally. This is especially true of autistic children.

May I Sit in Your Chair?

Summary

Students work as a group taking turns switching chairs.

This is an exercise in listening, taking turns, speaking up with confidence, and positive social interaction. The result is a continuing chain of students offering their places while relying on the group to help them get a new place.

Skills developed

- Sequencing, completing a task, turn taking, sharing, patience
- Listening, eye contact

Measures of success

- Make eye contact and actively observe
- Ask confidently and politely, and offer willingly
- Involve those who haven't had a turn yet
- Always answer "Yes," and support other students
- Follow the correct sequence of tasks

Procedure

1. Student A asks Student B if they can sit in Student B's chair.
2. Student B answers "Yes."
3. Student A stands behind Student B's chair and waits while Student B asks someone else for their chair.
4. After Student B leaves for the next chair, Student A sits in the free chair.
5. Continue sequence.
6. After students master the game, try having them ask by making eye contact and nodding for agreement.
7. End the activity by having someone ask you for your place and then taking an empty chair.

Variations

- Students can ask using names, as in "John, may I stand in your place?"
- Have students remember which place they're in before you start. When it's time to end the game, tell them to return to that place.

Comments

The most important part of this activity is to make eye contact and listen to one another. Remind students that they need to look for someone who is making eye contact. If a student wants to be picked, they need to make eye contact with the person looking for a new chair.

The answer is always "Yes." If students aren't up for saying "Yes," have them sit out of the circle until they're ready to participate.

Mirror

Summary

Students, in pairs, face each other and take turns following the other student's movements.

Skills developed

- Coordination, control
- Attention and observation
- Supporting and assisting others
- Accepting suggestions and guidance

Measures of success

- Observe and follow their partner
- Remain calm while focusing
- Lead in a way that their partner can follow

Procedure

1. Discuss how when you look in the mirror the image in the mirror moves the same as you do.
2. Pair up with another adult and demonstrate by having one person lead and the other one follow.
3. Have students form pairs and designate which of them leads and which one mirrors the other.
4. Remind them to lead in a way that the other can follow and that they'll switch off so that the other person will get the chance to lead.
5. Have the leader lead.
6. Switch leader and follower after a brief time.

Comments

It's important to remind students to keep the motion simple, smooth, and slow. Remind them that actors help each other and want to make the other person look good.

Magic Box

Summary

Students take turns pulling imaginary objects from an imaginary box. They can give them as gifts or have people guess what they are using or doing with the object.

Skills developed

- Physical coordination
- Miming skills
- Interference

Measures of success

- Demonstrate an object by using it clearly
- Join in guessing what other students are demonstrating

Procedure

1. Explain that you have a magic, invisible box.
2. Mime bringing out the magic box and open it.
3. Tell the group that you can find any good thing in the invisible box.
4. Pull out an object and mime using it.
5. Ask them to guess what the object is or what you're doing with it.
6. If no one guesses correctly after three guesses, tell the group what it is.
7. Next person gets a turn.

Comments

Keep students answering the actual question. For example, if the question is "What am I using?" get them to say, "baseball bat" instead of, "You're Hank Aaron." Encourage students to be specific. If no one can guess, encourage the student to show different ways to use it.

Keep the imagination items positive: no guns, drugs, dirty underwear, etc. You can avoid negative objects by having students ask what they would like to get as a present and have them take that thing out of the box.

For some students, you might use a box with pictures of objects that students can pick for suggestions.

I'm a Tree

Summary

Three actors work together to portray a scene by improvising objects in a location.

I'm a Tree is an engaging way to show students what they can do just using their imagination and how they can create locations for other improv work. This is also useful to have in reserve when the class is restless and needs to direct its energy.

Skills developed

- Creative expression, portraying characters, understanding relationships
- Teamwork

Measures of success

- Participate willingly
- Add components appropriate to the context
- Maintain focus on what the scene is about and continue to listen
- Transition to a new scene

Procedure

1. Gather students into a circle.
2. Tell them, "Let's work together to pretend that we're different objects. We start with someone pretending to be a tree, like this."
3. Take a tree position and say, "I'm a tree. Now what could you find near a tree?" Tell whoever volunteers to jump in and mimic that thing while saying, "I'm a [whatever they are]."
4. A third person joins and says what they are.
5. The person who started the scene states which person they are taking away, and they leave together.

6. After they leave, the remaining actor repeats what they are, and two other actors join in a new scene.
7. Continue with new scenes until done.

Comments

Often more than three students jump in. Depending on what you want from the group, you can allow more or not. If there are more than three, you can end the game by having all the students join the scene.

Sometimes the scene can be a starting point for a story. If something comes to mind, use your judgment about whether to segue into acting out a story.

Look What I Found

Summary

Students take turns using an everyday object as something else.

Skills developed

- Inference
- Self-confidence

Measures of success

- Imagine what the object could be
- Participate willingly

Procedure

1. Gather students into a circle.
2. Find an object in the room and place it in the middle of the circle.
3. To demonstrate, pick up the object, use it as what you imagine it to be, and then say, "Look what I found, a . . ." followed by the name of what you're imagining it to be. For example, you could pick up a pencil, use it like a rocket taking off, and then say, "Look what I found, a rocket."
4. Put the object back in the center and wait for someone else to take a turn.

Variations

- Instead of saying what the object is, the player uses it as the imagined object and then the others guess what it is.
- The player uses the object but says something they would say when using it. For example, the player imagines that the pencil is a rocket but says, "I'm going to the moon."

Comments

Change the object periodically. Things with a part that moves, such as a lever or flap, can work best.

"Once Upon a Time . . ." Story

Summary

Group creates a story by completing sentences that are the outline of a basic story structure with a beginning, story development, and ultimate resolution. Students can later rehearse and present the stories that they develop.

Skills developed

- Understanding story structure
- Sequential thinking
- Verbal communication
- Cooperative work
- Accepting and adding on to other people's ideas

Measures of success

- Complete sentences to make a logical story
- Discuss story
- Participate with the group

Procedure

1. Bring students into a group.
2. Have the following starters written down:

   Once upon a time . . .
   And every day . . .
   But then one day . . .

And because of that . . .
And ever since . . .

3. Introduce the material to the class.
   "Now we're going to use these beginnings of sentences to help us tell a story. First, let's read them."
   Have students read the sentences.
4. Work with other teachers to complete the sentences and demonstrate how to finish the story.
5. Remind students to listen to one another and think what could happen to the people in the story.
6. Have students create a story by completing the sentences. Call on students and guide them as needed.
7. Follow up by asking students about the story, what it means, or what they think that they would do.

Variation

Have students act out a story.

Extending the Scope

These games, activities, and other improv exercises can also be played at home and as company team-building activities and offsite meetings. When I've led these exercises at company events, team leaders have commented that they confirmed or discovered keen insights about individual group members that resulted in promotions, team rearrangements, and personnel changes.

PART FIVE

MOVING FORWARD WITH EXCELLENCE

How you speak supports thoughts, ideas, feelings, and emotions. Specific musical placement of the voice and body movement adds clarity to the message. An impactful speaking voice requires power and subtlety that is grounded and confident. How you stand, the muscles you engage, and the way you breathe with emotional clarity support your opinion and personal history. Without a clear focus, the voice can sound weak, thin, too high, or too low. Placement of your hands can impact the success of your message, too.

Finding your voice, conveying emotion, capturing and holding an audience's attention, telling your story, trusting the power of suggestion, balancing the rhetorical triangle, and motivating an audience to think, feel, and take action requires a bit of work. With practice, it can become natural and instinctive.

This section features ways to blend and incorporate what you read and practiced earlier in this book.

There's comfort in doing things the same way. Shaking it up and trying other approaches keeps it fresh. Here's how to reframe your thought process if you find yourself getting stuck.

- Redefine "fear" as "excitement."
- Visualize success.
- Don't try to be perfect.
- Transform anxiety into confidence.
- Explore new performance options.

PUTTING IT ALL TOGETHER

Taking information out of the brain and into the body isn't as easy as it sounds. The analytical side of the brain likes to block creativity and trust in oneself. *Speak to Achieve* allows you to explore, make mistakes, take risks, and enjoy being you.

> **"The most powerful person in the world is the storyteller. The storyteller sets the vision, values, and agendas of an entire generation that is to come."**
>
> **—Steve Jobs**

CHAPTER 1

Personalizing Your Message

It's not all about the voice. It's about what makes *you* special.

- *Your* imagination.
- *Your* life experiences.
- *Your* sense of humor.
- *Your* interpretation of the message.
- How *you* use your body to make the words come alive.
- How *you* emotionally connect with the message.
- How much *you* believe that what you're saying is true.

Sharing Your Imagination: Bringing imagination to life and sharing it through words, feelings, and body language should inspire, captivate, and resonate with your audience. It can create a sense of wonder and curiosity, encourage visualization and involvement, and convey abstract concepts in relatable and memorable ways. Yet many adults struggle with tapping into their "inner child," who envisioned an environment and created dialogue for themselves and their toys.

Actors use imagination to bring a character to life, and so must a speaker. These two jobs overlap in that both rely on envisioning scenes, emotions, and vivid details to create compelling and authentic experiences for their audiences.

Actor's Imagination: Actors use imagination to create a backstory, immerse their character in that world, visualize settings, and define relationships. They access a range of emotions based on the character's imagined history, perspectives, and opinions. Actors tell stories through their characters by using imagination to make each role unique and believable. They embody their character through physicality, gestures, posture, and facial expressions.

Actors strive to draw audiences into their imagined world and feel as if they're part of the story.

Speaker's Imagination: Speakers build a world for their audience by bringing abstract ideas to life through vivid descriptions and detailed imagery. They evoke impactful feelings that authentically resonate with their audience. Speakers shape their story by infusing it with personal meaning and detail. By animating their physical presence, speakers adopt the body language, tone, and energy needed to enhance the message. Expressing ideas that foster a deeper connection and shared understanding, speakers strive to include the audience to become co-creators of the experience.

Using Your Life Experiences: Memories help speakers connect emotionally with the message as they share personal stories, encourage audiences to reflect on their own experiences, and relate the speaker's story to their own lives. Actors use a technique called "substitution" to bring a script to life by understanding the meaning and depth of the dialogue, accessing corresponding personal experiences and emotions, and blending the two to authentically portray their character's feelings and actions.

Using substitution builds a foundation for embodying a believable character in addition to delivering an evocative speech. Here's a system that speakers can follow:

- Identify emotions and experiences in the message that you want the audience to resonate with like joy, empathy, excitement, trust, fear, anger, and humor.
- Find personal parallels to that emotional moment in your own life.
- If you can relate directly to that experience, then use it. If not, imagine a "what if?" scenario that viscerally accesses that emotion.
- Use the substitution as a starting point to blend personal emotion with the context, motive, purpose, and role of the speaking job.
- Recall and channel physical sensations and sensory cues.
- Truly experience the emotional journey that intertwines the job requirements and your personal life.

Adding Your Sense of Humor: Everyone loves a good laugh, especially when they're laughing *with* you and not *at* you. A speaker needs to "read the room," be adaptable, and tailor the humor to audience demographics, cultural background, context, and type of event. There are many ways to incorporate humor into your speech.

- Share lighthearted stories, relatable experiences, everyday mishaps, misunderstandings, or minor personal failings that resonate with others and show your human side.
- Make gentle fun of yourself to lighten the mood and put the audience at ease.
- Use observational humor to point out funny or absurd aspects of everyday situations.
- Add witty remarks, one-liners, and punchlines for quick humor that doesn't derail the main message.
- Incorporate wordplay, words with double meanings, and puns to add a touch of lightheartedness and charm.
- Exaggerate a reaction to highlight an experience or frustration.
- Use timing and pauses effectively to let the punchline land.
- If appropriate, include funny visuals or props to complement the joke or story.

Your Interpretative Spin on the Message: Personalization helps audiences connect with the speaker's individuality and see the topic through a new, distinct lens. Nuance and understanding, insight and opinion, passion and emotion, tone and style are expressions of a unique perspective.

- Highlight unusual connections to creatively draw unrelated ideas or concepts together.
- Choose analogies and metaphors that resonate in a personal and meaningful way to bring the topic closer to the audience.
- Infuse emotion and passion to influence the tone and impact of the message.
- Authentically align the topic with your core beliefs.

- Ask thought-provoking questions that challenge conventional thinking or invite reflection.
- Choose a tone and style that conveys your personality and unique interpretation on the subject.
- Invite the audience to explore the topic and reflect on how it applies to their lives.

Allow Your Body to Make the Words Come Alive: Combining body movement, voice, expression, and words creates a multi-sensory impact that helps a speaker connect more profoundly with their audience. Physical expression brings energy, emotion, and emphasis to spoken words. If it's time to talk and you're feeling tired or resistant to movement, quickly address the problem. Stretch, jump up and down, dance, wiggle, twist, or perform some other form of exercise to unlock the body and allow it to bring your words to life.

The message comes alive when you:

- Make movements purposeful.
- Follow the GPS behind the words to physically mirror emotions, locations, and actions.
- Use the word emphasis chart to add focus to important words and phrases.
- Define the size and shape of your power box gesture area and keep your movements inside that imaginary space.
- Belief what you're saying.
- Let movements help the message come alive.

Believe What You Say: A speaker who believes what they're saying inspires others to believe in it too. A stronger connection is built when passion and authenticity shine through. But speakers often have "tells" that send a mixed message that the speaker isn't genuinely connected with certain elements.

Here's a checklist for believing in your message and delivering it with conviction and authenticity.

Believability Checklist

- ❑ Understand the core purpose and *why* your message matters.
- ❑ Connect to personal values and experiences.
- ❑ Reframe doubts or concerns in a positive way.
- ❑ Practice emotional visualization.
- ❑ Familiarize yourself with evidence, stories, or examples to reinforce the message.
- ❑ Align the message with your personal and professional goals.
- ❑ Take time to self-reflect and affirm your belief in the message.
- ❑ Think about the potential benefits and positive impact for the audience.
- ❑ Speak from the heart, be true to yourself, and embrace authenticity.

CHAPTER 2

Developing Your Style

Very few people are naturally engaging speakers. Achieving a personal speaking style takes time, practice, and self-discovery. Here are some suggestions on how to blend your unique personality, natural strengths, and interests into a communication style that represents who you are and what you want to achieve.

YOUR STRENGTHS AND WEAKNESSES

Your first assignment in the Introduction was to write down five of your top strengths and five of your primary weaknesses.

Are you a good storyteller, have a strong speaking voice, listen well, move and gesture effectively, consistently prepare, practice diligently, trust yourself, are confident, humorous, empathetic, relatable, adaptable, authoritative, engaging, genuine and open, etc.?

Strength: When a speaker relies too heavily on a strength, it can become a weakness. The speaker may become lazy, repetitive, automatic, facile, or push too hard. When that happens, the strength moves into the weakness category. This is why it's important to improve our weaknesses, so they rise up to the quality and benefits of the strengths.

What about your weaknesses? Do you need to improve your pacing, diction, voice placement, organizational skills, speaking and movement coordination, speech structure, comfort and naturalness, etc.?

Weakness: Acknowledging and improving weaknesses takes effort. That's why people tend to rely on their tried-and-true strengths. But perfection can be boring. Audiences connect with imperfections, too. So don't be afraid to acknowledge where you're not strong. And if you want to move a weakness into the strength category, practice and improve the area you feel needs work.

BODY-MOVEMENT-VOICE

Coordinating movement, gestures, and speech can feel like patting your head and rubbing your tummy. The poor brain has to increase its cognitive load with the dual task of managing the language centers for speech *and* the cerebellum and motor cortex for movement. Sprinkle in a little nervousness or anxiety, and it can become difficult to synchronize timing, rhythm, and movement with necessary word or phrase emphasis.

Practice and rehearsal develop muscle memory, so the brain doesn't have to think about the movements anymore. When gestures and movements are natural and organically support the message, the speaker is "wired for sound."

If you're having trouble in a particular area, slow down the movements and words. Practice the movements like you would a new dance step. Repeat the coordinated movement and words in ultra-slow motion. As the voice and body connection becomes second nature and fully ingrained, increase the speech and movement speed until it's at the tempo you desire.

Performance note: The goal is to have natural gestures align with the rhythm and emphasis of speech. If you have to *think* about what or how to say or move, keep practicing. You want to be out of your head and in your body.

SPEAKING STYLES

Knowing your audience and the goal is key to selecting the appropriate speaking style. Each style has a unique body language, tone, and delivery. Below is a description of sixteen speaking styles. Feel free to select and use one of them or blend a few together. For fun, you may want to close your eyes and randomly point to three different styles. Then, find a way to create a speech that ties all three of those styles together. Creativity comes from challenging yourself.

1. **Extemporaneous**: Conversational, casual, partially prepared
2. **Informative**: Educational and explanatory
3. **Entertaining**: Amusing, engaging, enjoyable
4. **Persuasive**: Engaging, motivational, passionate
5. **Formal:** Structured and measured
6. **Informal:** Relaxed and conversational
7. **Impromptu**: Unexpected, spontaneous, unscripted

8. **Oratorical**: Formal, structured, inspirational
9. **Debate**: Argumentative, logical, competitive
10. **Ceremonial**: Emotional, reflective, uplifting
11. **Narrative**: Storytelling, expressive, anecdotal
12. **Demonstrative**: Hands-on, explaining, guiding
13. **Comedic**: Humorous, unexpected, relatable, relies on timing, delivery, pacing
14. **Compassionate**: Positive, heartfelt, reassuring, empathetic, supportive
15. **Evocative**: Expressive, emotionally charged
16. **Conversational**: Natural, interactive, casual

Natural or Awkward: Knowing if a message "lands" relies on both the speaker's internal cues and external audience feedback. Performing outside one's comfort zone may feel awkward at first. With practice it can become natural, easy, and instinctive. So don't give up!

- Record yourself practicing or delivering the actual speech.
- Identify times that you are relaxed and genuine.
- Pinpoint moments that appear stiff or disconnected.
- Ask yourself why: Is it the content that needs refinement, movements, pacing changes, delivery style adjustment, voice placement, etc.?
- Through self-awareness you can reduce awkwardness, enhance your natural presence, and refine your speaking style.

SPEAKER RESEARCH

Comedian Benny Hill once quipped: "I've always said, if you can take a joke from one man, it's stealing. If you take it from many, it's research." While there's a fine line between influence and plagiarism, ideas evolve through inspiration and adaptation to make it your own. Watch, analyze, and "borrow" specific elements in speech, structure, movement, and delivery style that resonate with you. If unsure where and what to look for, here's a list of resources and platforms where you can observe and analyze speaker techniques, delivery styles, and audience engagement methods.

- **TED and TEDx Talks**: TED.com offers a collection of engaging and well-prepared experts and thought leaders across a wide range of fields. Its database can be searched by topic, style, or speaker.
- **YouTube**: Search by famous speakers, specific types of events, or speech genres to find countless videos in every speaking style.
- **Public Speaking Events and Conferences**: Attend in-person and online events to see speakers of all skill levels present at industry conferences and local speaking clubs.
- **Resources and Tips**: Websites like Toastmasters.com and Speaking.com offer resources, public speaking tips, and a list of notable speakers.
- **Podcasts**: Listen, watch, and subscribe to podcasts that feature interviews, stories, and talks from a variety of speakers.
- **Audiobooks**: Study the tone, tempo, and storytelling techniques of well-known speakers, actors, and authors.
- **Social Media**: Select and follow specific speakers on platforms like LinkedIn, Instagram, and TikTok to get quick insights on a variety of speaking styles and approaches.
- **Streaming Services**: Platforms like Netflix, Amazon Prime, and Hulu offer documentaries and stand-up comedy specials that showcase various speaking styles.

EMBRACE YOUR STYLE

How and what you speak about should reflect your unique personality, values, perspective, subject knowledge, and status. Staying true to oneself will be different for everyone. One speaker might embrace their quirks, humor, and vulnerabilities while another speaker may prefer a more formal, polished, and precise approach.

- Finding your style is a gradual process.
- Allow yourself to be open to new techniques, styles, and speaking opportunities.
- Stay true to yourself and be aware that your style isn't static.

- Your speaking style will evolve and grow as you gain more experience.
- Over time, you'll get a handle on what works best in specific situations and with different audiences.

CHAPTER 3

Storytelling

Businesses often favor storytelling speakers because they deliver more than information. They engage audiences, create an emotional connection, and make complex ideas relatable. Storytelling speakers appeal to a wide range of audiences by using a narrative story arc that:

- Inspires and motivates
- Enhances the company's brand and culture
- Encourages action
- Drives change and innovation

Storytelling encompasses many styles and genres. Choosing the right storytelling style depends on the message content, strength and adaptability of the speaker, goal for the target audience, and the performance medium where it occurs. Based on a speaker's strengths and weaknesses the scope of choices will narrow or broaden. You may want to put a checkmark by the ones you feel most comfortable using or would like to learn or improve.

Select Your Storytelling Style

- ❑ Traditional straightforward, linear narrative
- ❑ Nonlinear narrative where the story jumps around in time
- ❑ Episodic storytelling with smaller, mini-arc, or standalone segments that contribute to a larger narrative
- ❑ "Frame" story where the main story encompasses one or more secondary stories
- ❑ First-person narrative

(Continued.)

- ❑ Third-person omniscient
- ❑ Stream of consciousness
- ❑ Dialogue-driven narrative showcasing conversations with other people
- ❑ Self-reflective or meditative thoughts and insights
- ❑ Interactive audience participation
- ❑ Visual using photographs, illustrations, film, and body language to tell the story
- ❑ Poetic language, rhythm, and metaphor that emphasizes mood, symbolism, and sensory experiences
- ❑ Allegory, parable, symbolic, or metaphorical tale to convey a moral, lesson, or deeper meaning
- ❑ Improvisational, incorporating spontaneous audience reactions and contributions
- ❑ Epic or mythic larger-than-life tales rooted in cultural myths, legends, or historical events

CHAPTER 4

Dividing the Workload into Three Sections

The "Rule of Three" is an effective way to structure and deliver a message with a story arc that includes a beginning, middle, and end.

1. Set up the problem.
2. Knock down the problem by offering solutions.
3. Send the follow-up message out to the audience so they feel empowered to take action on it.

Dividing the workload into three sections is also a way to define the Speaker "3-P" work areas:

1. Preparation
2. Performance
3. Post Analysis

Whether you're doing all the work yourself or outsourcing some of it, there are challenges to overcome.

- Identify the problem.
- Define the message in one word.
- Prioritize key message points.
- Select supporting stories and examples.
- Identify the "rule of three" transitions.
- Practice, adapt, and stay flexible.
- Enjoy the performance experience.
- Be open to suggestions and critiques.

CHAPTER 5

Emotional Colors of Speech

Using the "emotional colors" of speech leverages vocal tone, pace, volume, and body language to evoke and convey an array of emotions throughout a presentation. Variety is dynamic and ever changing, which helps captivate and hold the audience's attention. Whether you deliver your message like a painter who knows all the colors and shadings, see the words like a musician hears music, or connect with the emotional variety of words in your own unique way is your personal choice. The only wrong choice is no choice.

Vary the Tone to Reflect Different Emotions

- Warm and inviting
- Excited and upbeat
- Serious and grave
- Curious and inquisitive

Adjust your Pacing to Match Emotional Intensity

- Slow down for emphasis and reflection.
- Speed up to convey excitement or urgency.
- Use pauses to build suspense and emphasis.
- Add timing changes for comedic effect.

Modulate Volume to Enhance Emotional Contrast

- Speak louder to project assertiveness or passion.
- Speak softer to create a sense of intimacy or reflection.
- Use crescendos and decrescendos to mimic the rise and fall of emotional intensity.

Incorporate Body Language and Facial Expressions

- Use open gestures for ease, warmth, and enthusiasm.
- Leverage facial expressions to convey emotions.
- Adapt physical stances, movements, and gestures to the emotional context.

Select Words that Evoke Specific Emotions

- Choose vivid, descriptive, emotional language.
- Incorporate stories, personal anecdotes, and examples that resonate emotionally.

Tailor Emotional Colors to the Audience

- **Understand the Audience's Emotional Landscape**—An intimate setting might call for warmth and sincerity. Yet those "emotional colors" may not be appreciated in a business setting where the more receptive choice is inspiration and confidence.
- **Match Emotional Colors to the Message's Purpose**—Rather than painting in one emotional color, add variety so the different parts of the speech express different emotional tones and colors.

CHAPTER 6

Truth or "Tell"

Poker players are watched carefully by their opponents to see if they show any conscious or unconscious signs about the strength or weakness of their cards. While audiences may not identify the cause of what's not resonating with them, they too often feel message disconnects and conflicts. So, recognizing your own "tells" and knowing how to adjust them into "truths" is a powerful and persuasive tool to store in the speaker's toolbelt.

Unconscious "tells" are baked into our DNA. Unwanted body movement and vocal changes can take over during a speech, reading, or performance, too. The "tell" may be the result of feeling underprepared or uncomfortable in the environment, having to speak on a new or unfamiliar topic, shyness, reading or presenting someone else's words, or the perceived self-doubt and fraudulence of one's abilities and accomplishments that encourages "imposter syndrome." In all these cases, the body can react as if the speaker is telling a lie.

These untruthful "tells" in the voice, body, and overall message can adversely affect the desired result. Below are some signs that your body is reacting to what it perceives to be a lie and the adjustments you can make to connect with your truth and your ability to speak so the audience accepts what you're saying.

RECOGNIZING THE TELL

Let's take a look at ways the body reacts when it perceives a lie, bluff, or untruth.

1. The pitch of the voice goes up and is higher than normal. This can be throughout the whole message or on specific words, phrases, or sections.

2. The speaker steps back to create distance from the individual, audience, or microphone.
3. Broad sweeping hand gestures are used to create distance away from their body. This is the brain's way of creating distance from the lie.
4. In anticipation of questions, direction, or comments the speaker steps back or out of the performance space and into a safer area.
5. Head movement and verbal response is the opposite of that body movement. For example, nodding "yes" while saying the opposite word "no."
6. Vocal inflection may be loud, erratic, harsh, or in the wrong places.
7. Sounding flat, noncommittal, neutral, or bland.
8. Emotional disconnection throughout the message or in specific sections.
9. Authority and opinion are not established.

PROJECTING THE TRUTH

Here are some lie-to-truth steps to support the message and present the information in a truthful and believable manner.

1. To lower the pitch, shake out the arms and legs, breathe deeply a few times, place one or both hands on your heart, and listen to your body as you feel it relax.
2. Own the space around and under you by stretching your arms out and planting your heels or stomping them in the ground.
3. Gesture forward with one hand. With the opposite hand, point to yourself.
4. Move both hands forward with the thumbs up. Then, turn your hands over so the palms face up.
5. Rather than stepping back, stay in the same location. You may want to lean forward or bend a knee to relax one leg.
6. In front of a mirror, practice nodding "yes" while saying the positive message and shaking the head "no" when stating

information, people, or things you don't believe are true or as good as you or your message content.

7. Don't think about individual word stress. Instead, focus on the purpose and truth of the full message. Once you know WHY you're saying something, volume and tone issues tend to even out and support the message.
8. Vocal warmups and singing lessons improve speech musicality. Play different styles of music when practicing a speech, interview, or reading a script. Notice how the music brings the message to life differently depending on the music's energy, tempo, style, and mood.
9. Emotion supports opinion. Look for and use little words that are sprinkled throughout the script, message, or story to establish your authority and how you feel about the logical information being discussed.
10. Create a mantra for yourself that centers you and encourages confidence to share your authority and opinion. It could be a word or sound that is repeated or a statement or slogan. For example, when I'm uncertain, I repeat a mantra like this silently in my head: "Breathe . . . smile . . . you got this!"

Truth and Tell Assignment

List three "tells" you believe you may project to your audience.

1. ______________________________
2. ______________________________
3. ______________________________

List three "truth" adjustments that you're going to start practicing and using now.

1. ______________________________
2. ______________________________
3. ______________________________

Create a mantra that you can use to encourage permission to get out of your way and into the truth of your message, body, and voice.

____

____

When you start detecting deception and discrepancies in your body and voice, you can use these tools to turn inconsistent messaging into powerful truths!

CHAPTER 7

Trusting the Techniques

Improving verbal and nonverbal communication skills are essential for both personal and professional growth. As such, you can't just *read* a personal development book to improve, you have to *practice* the techniques. When practicing, consider how each technique aligns with your personal needs and goals.

Check the boxes that represent reasons why you want to *Speak to Achieve*.

Speak to Achieve Checklist

- ❑ Build confidence and self-trust
- ❑ Express yourself more clearly and assertively
- ❑ Leadership and authority
- ❑ Career advancement
- ❑ Interviews and negotiations
- ❑ Interpersonal expression to understand others better
- ❑ Optimize understanding and applying how the voice, body, and mind work together
- ❑ Reduce conflicts
- ❑ Increase sales
- ❑ Emotional intelligence for using and reading body language, emotions, and tone
- ❑ Comfort in public speaking
- ❑ Persuasive speaking

As you practice, you may want to break each technique down into tiny bits that add up to a final performance. When you encounter a difficult section, practice slowly, create muscle memory, and make course corrections as needed. Some techniques will come easily, while others may take more time to naturally and instinctively incorporate and use.

CHAPTER 8

Practice: Body Language

By now you should realize that the body shares information and gives away secrets on how we feel. How we stand and position our bodies can also send mixed messages. For instance, hands clasped together low and in front of the body in a "fig leaf" position can appear withdrawn, avoiding, and covering up. "Dead arms" that droop to the sides of the body can come off as lifeless and disengaged. "Crossed arms" in front of the body can appear defensive, disconnected, and detached. Some of these so-called negative positions can also be used well. When deciding how to engage and present information, consider these body language techniques.

ARMS

- **Standing**: Hands together with steepled fingers or hands cupped on top of each other.
- **Talking**: Alternating gestures within an appropriate gesture size area.
- **Drawing Focus Elsewhere**: Angle the body and drop the hands to the "fig leaf" position to draw focus *away* from oneself and to another location.
- **Strong Posture**: When the shoulders are back, spine is straight, and feet are hip width apart, the arms can be by the sides to communicate confidence and presence.
- **Crossed Arms**: Used sparingly and briefly, crossed arms can be used when thinking or in a transitional moment.

SHOULDERS

- **Straight shoulders** present logical information—Presentation, information, discussion, business interview, negotiation.
- **One shoulder** angled toward the audience conveys attitude, emotion, and opinion—Meeting, discussion, presentation.
- **Relaxed shoulders** show confidence—Calming, presentation posture.
- **Leading with the heart with shoulders back** shows openness—Allows air in, opens up the rib cage, and drops the shoulders back and down.
- **Leaning forward with both shoulders** indicates interest, engagement, action, and valuing input. Be aware: if used extensively you could be perceived as coming on too strong.
- **An aggressive stance with shoulders back** and chest out—Intimidation.
- **Leaning the shoulders back** displays confidence or detachment depending on your expression and attitude.

FEET

- **Whether walking or standing**, your feet can ground, focus, and relax you or they can project that you're tense or nervous.
- **Remain still** on important keywords and phrases.
- **Move on less important** connecting thoughts or actions.
- **The position** of your feet influences your presentation.
- **Parallel feet** project confidence and control.
- **Narrow versus wide** stances should be decided on based on the message in that moment.
- **Beware of swaying** and rocking back and forth. To avoid this, put your weight on your heels and stay planted and grounded.
- **Avoid pointing your toes inward**. Pigeon toes can make you appear unsure and unconfident.
- **Feet in an 11-and-1 o'clock position** creates a dynamic that brings the speaker closer to your audience, allows comfortable weight shift from foot to foot, and minimizes swaying.

EYES

- **Eyes tell others how you feel**, whether concerned or relieved, engaged or disconnected, nervous or confident, imagining or remembering.
- **Be interested and engaged**. Don't stare the person or audience down.
- **It's okay to kinesthetically look away** to think, process, imagine, create, or recall memories or feelings.

CHAPTER 9

Practice: Gestures and Movements

An engaging speaker uses purposeful arm gestures to connect with the audience. In most cases, you want to gesture from the waist up. It's best to raise the hands to waist level and gesture out using one or both hands. Reserve the use of both hands to simultaneously gesture on the most important information.

- **Verbs**: Gesture with movement on action words.
- **Stationary Nouns**: Point and hold a gesture in the direction of a location, person, or object.
- **Active Nouns**: Simulate the movement of an object, person, place, or thing if it actively moves from one location to another.

It's easy to get in your head and allow self-doubt to creep in. Add movement to get out of the head and into the body.

- Start with a physical movement or "body pop."
- Physicalize emotions.

CHAPTER 10

Practice: Logic, Emotion, and Authority

Consider using the rhetorical triangle to balance your message. Remember that logical information also needs emotion to establish opinion and authority. When a message is neutral, it lacks history, persuasion, a personal connection, and a reason for speaking. Using happy and sad as opposing goal posts and the spectrum of emotions in between, speakers and storytellers establish their authority by sharing their personal feelings, opinions, and logical information.

- Logically organize your message with a clear beginning, middle, and end.
- Emotionally engage your audience with a relatable, universal theme, and story arc.
- Establish authority, trust, and credibility before diving into the story or message.

Use the Rhetorical Triangle to craft a strong speech, message, or story.

- Begin with *ethos* to lay the foundational connection.
- Use *pathos* to build audience investment in the outcome.
- Incorporate *logos* to tie the information all together by connecting evidence, facts, and reasoning.

CHAPTER 11

Practice: Voice and Speech

It's not practice makes perfect but *perfect practice* makes perfect. Finding the perfect set of exercises to warm up the voice and improve speech may include diction, resonance, breathing, pitch, speaking range, placement, and volume exercises. Pacing, tempo, timing, pausing, and inflection may also need attention. What about speech musicality, building the message out, and emotional effectiveness? All of these areas are addressed in this book. Revisit those targeted areas as you wish to improve your voice and performance.

It's important to protect your vocal health. If you experience any vocal stress or discomfort, here are some suggestions to relieve stress and prevent further damage. If vocal fatigue, strain, or injury persist, consult a speech-language pathologist or an otolaryngologist (ear-nose-throat specialist) for treatment and rehabilitation.

- **Rest Your Voice**: When your voice is fatigued, refrain from speaking, whispering, or singing to allow time for your vocal cords to recover.
- **Hydrate Frequently**: Drinking water throughout the day, especially one hour before speaking, lubricates the vocal cords and reduces irritation.
- **Avoid Clearing Your Throat**: In addition to straining the voice, this repeated action can cause the voice to change pitch, clarity, and create a persistent pattern of irritation. Instead, gently cough, swallow, hum, or drink a sip of water.
- **Prepare Your Voice for Speaking**: Create a voice exercise routine that begins gently and builds to more vigorous exercises.
- **Speak from the Diaphragm**: Keep your shoulders down and breathe up from the belly that takes air in and out. Avoid

speaking from the chest—that employs shallow breaths that lift the shoulders up and down.

- **Talk on the Airflow**: Allow a tiny bit of air to expel through the mouth before speaking, then talk along with that airflow to support and produce the sound.
- **Soothe Your Throat**: Drink warm herbal teas with lemon or honey (propolis honey is my favorite), suck on throat lozenges without menthol, or inhale steam.

WARM UP THE BODY

The voice isn't the only area that needs to warm up before speaking. The body also needs to be woken up and engaged. Listen to your body. There may be days that your voice is warmed up already or you only need a quick warm-up, and other days that you need to repeat each warm-up exercise multiple times.

Here are a few face and body warm-ups:

- Warm up the face by pretending that you're biting and chewing an apple.
- Roll your shoulders forward, up, and back. Circle them around in both directions.
- Drop your ear to your shoulder, then repeat this motion on the other side.
- Lower your chin to your chest and hold it for five or ten seconds.
- Shake your hands and then your arms.
- Shake each foot and leg.
- Stomp your heels into the ground.
- Breathe in from the toes up to the head and release the air out slowly.

CHAPTER 12

Practice: Script Techniques

Crafting your speech so that it's compelling, clear, and impactful adds to its engagement, connection with the audience, and lasting impression. Whether scripted by you or someone else, or relying on notes to improvise or extemporize the message, practice using these techniques.

- Minimize emphasizing "I." Instead, focus on "you" and "we" by gesturing out to create a sense of connection.
- Have a clear beginning, middle, and end that ties the key elements together.
- Define the primary takeaway that you want your audience to remember.
- Practice or mark your script with pauses, emotional transitions, emojis, or word emphasis symbols that draw focus to important elements and encourage active listening.
- Create compelling openings and closings that set you apart from the crowd.
- Embody the message with subtext and actions instead of words alone.

CHAPTER 13

What Kind of Authority Are You?

Defining the category of authority a speaker fits into helps solidify the information, context, delivery style, and interaction with the audience. Authority figures can range from familiar and casual to distant and removed. Or from heartfelt and giving to indifferent and cold. Depending on the job and situation, the type of authority changes.

Below are ten specific authority types with different sources, implications, and power of influence. This is useful in understanding your role and why people act a particular way in social, political, and organizational contexts.

- **Charismatic leaders** inspire others and generate enthusiasm.
- **Traditional leaders** have inherited power or customs, traditions, and accepted practices passed down through generations.
- **Rational-Legal authorities** are tied to the position a person holds and the formal rules and regulations of that bureaucratic and modern organization.
- **Expert authorities** are recognized for their knowledge, skills, and expertise.
- **Positional authority** is based on hierarchy and title, role, or position within a company or institution.
- **Moral authorities** are seen as ethical, having integrity and high moral standing.
- **Informal authorities** arise naturally within a group based on admiration, respect, and influence.
- **Coercive authorities** compel behavior through force, threat of punishment, power, and control.

- **Persuasive authorities** persuade, convince, and influence others through argument, reasoning, and emotional appeal.
- **Delegated authority** is transferred from one person or group to another.

CHAPTER 14

Score Your Speech Success

Now that you've read and practiced the exercises in this book, take a moment to score your speech success. Rate yourself on a scale of one to five, with one being the lowest score and five the highest. Then, tally your score and compare it to a score you might have given yourself before reading this book.

Don't forget the four key elements in Making It M.I.N.E., especially the need. Make a choice. Be specific. Select the one word that resonates with you and your audience that will deliver the desired result. Your audience needs that clarity.

SCORE YOUR SPEECH SUCCESS FROM ONE TO FIVE IN EACH CATEGORY

______ **Defining the one-word NEED** and using it as a throughline to connect with the audience and leave a clear, lasting impression and call-to-action.

______ **Identifying the MOTIVATION** that relates to the audience and connects emotionally and imaginatively to a specific personal experience.

______ **Using active INTENTIONS** in movements and gestures to clarify, define, and show intent.

______ **Adding EMOTIONS** to establish your unique point of view, opinion, and authority.

______ **Trusting YOURSELF** to deliver the message in a meaningful and purposeful way.

______**TOTAL SCORE**

While speech communication is often described as a "soft skill," it's one of the most powerful tools a person can possess. Verbal and nonverbal communication is used every day, in all areas of personal and business life. Make the most of it!

Adopt the mantra: I can *Speak to Achieve*!

Epilogue

In capturing my experiences over the years to share in this book, I searched through interviews where I'm quoted and articles that I've written. I was astounded by how an article I wrote some years ago for *The Hindu Business Line* sums up the "strategies to make your communication intelligent and engaging."

Let me back up for a moment to put this in context. After several coaching sessions with a Silicon Valley businessman, he told me he was moving to India to start a company and was going to bring me over to help. Lo and behold, a few months later, he did! He asked me to write several communication training modules for his company to film and promote. Over the course of two weeks, I performed as the on-camera narrator, directed a couple local actors to demonstrate the techniques, and flew from Chennai to Bangalore to lead a full-day conference with what appeared to me to be the CEOs of all the major companies in India. During this time, I was written up in about a dozen newspapers and lauded as the "Communication Guru."

With only a few minor changes from the original article, here's what I wrote:

ADD SOME ZING TO YOUR COMMUNICATION

A good presentation should take the audience on a journey.

Requirements for corporate employees and executives have changed dramatically over the years. It's no longer adequate to sit in an office or cubicle and do the work. The new business paradigm has added "show" to the résumé. Expectations are high. Attention spans are short. Time is precious. And presentations and communications must reflect this business paradigm by being interesting and engaging, as well as intelligent.

Didn't sign up to be an actor? Left-brained analytical thinkers are required to perform right-brain creative tasks. Steve Jobs, co-founder of Apple and Pixar Animation Studios, while not an actor, set the performance bar high. He was comfortable in front of an audience, enthusiastic about his products, interacted well with support media, addressed technical issues, embraced competition head-on in a humorous way, and took audiences on an emotional journey.

Three Pillars

When assembling information for emails, phone calls, in-house meetings, webinars, seminars, sales presentations, podcasts, blogs, videos, conferences, e-learning modules, and tradeshows, three main rhetorical elements are essential—ethos, logos, and pathos. Ethos establishes authority; the reason why you speak and audiences listen. Logos is the logical reason and content. Pathos is the emotional component that moves the audience to take action viscerally.

Handing out a business card or stating a name and position in the company do not automatically establish ethos. Body language, voice modulation, confidence, and passion create an aura of authority that bring audiences to a speaker and make audiences want to listen. Logos, when presented in succinct, organized headlines and bullet points, is easy to assimilate. The more verbose, unstructured, and rambling a presentation, the less likely listeners are to take action. Pathos is the emotional bridge between the speaker and the audience. This emotional through-line gives the message purpose.

Every story has three sections: situational setup, body of information, and resolution or call to action. The setup establishes authority (ethos) and the reason why we deserve the product or service (pathos). The body of the presentation is primarily composed of logic (logos) mixed with a little authority (ethos), as content is defined and clarified. Emotion (pathos) is sprinkled in strategically to connect with the listener. Finally, pathos and ethos unite in the concluding statements to confirm a positive feeling about the speaker and the product or service. Logos is used to summarize information.

Problems

If we understand that communication is a story that includes ethos, logos, and pathos, why is it difficult for speakers to achieve communication perfection? Discomfort in front of a group, fear of public speaking, disorganization, lack of conviction, and low self-confidence wreak psychological havoc on many presenters. These insecurities manifest in stutters and stammers, inappropriate or repeated comments, foot shuffling, rocking motions, poor eye contact, and closed body positions. Al Franken, who created "Daily Affirmations" hosted by his character Stuart Smalley on the television show *Saturday Night Live,* had a mantra for dealing with these insecurities: "I'm good enough, I'm smart enough, and doggone it, people like me."

By taking a few slow grounding breaths, relaxing the body, and reminding ourselves of our self-worth before we begin speaking, many of the insecurities that live inside us rescind and allow confidence in.

Albert Mehrabian, known for his pioneering work in the field of nonverbal communication, developed the "7 percent–38 percent–55 percent Rule." In face-to-face communication, three elements account for the meaning of the message: Words, 7 percent; tone of voice, 38 percent; and body language, 55 percent. All three areas must support one another for the message to be congruent. If a person has excellent verbal content but avoids eye contact, shifts weight repeatedly, and has a closed body position, the listener is less likely to accept or fully comprehend the information.

When we approach communication, we need to select our emotional end result. Do we want the listener to be relieved, amused, concerned, proud, confident, entertained, inspired, or motivated? That emotional through-line helps define our body position and creates vocal nuances. For most people who make presentations, the majority of the time is spent preparing content rather than defining the emotional pain point. Therefore, how one makes a presentation is often an afterthought. Here are some suggestions:

Define the emotional problem. Is it frustration, lack of confidence, anxiousness, or nervousness? (Select one)

Define the solution. Is it ease, confidence, pride, or calm? (Select one)

State the understanding of the problem. For example, "I understand we have a tight time constraint to get the product to market." In this acknowledgment, the presenter can hold a little tenseness in the body. This establishes the emotional link between the presenter and the listener's concerns.

Emotional arc. The content of the message should now chip away at the pain point, guiding the listener from dis-ease to ease. Vocally and visually, the presenter becomes more and more relaxed and fluid with each new bit of information.

Calm, confident closing. No tenseness is in the body. The presenter's shoulders are back. There's a personable smile on the face and a confident twinkle in the eye. When successful, the listener appears relieved and confident too.

Emotions lie in the breath. It is what ties one sentence to the next. When afraid or nervous, breaths are quick, shallow, and quivery. A quick gasp of air happens when suddenly surprised. Breathing is deep and slow when relaxed. A sigh is often a sign of relief. Pay attention to breathing. Shallow breaths often signify tenseness, nervousness, or dissatisfaction. Slow deep breaths are contemplative and accepting.

Communication is a reciprocal event. It involves talking and watching. Pay attention not only to yourself, but your listener's vocal and body signals. Adjust to change. Take the listener on an emotionally arced journey. Think when you prepare the information. Feel when you communicate it. And remember, good listeners are just as valuable as good speakers.

Acknowledgments

A special thanks to my publisher, Tad Crawford, for the opportunity to publish this third speech communication book together. *Speak to Achieve*, aimed at business and personal use, completes the speech communication book trilogy alongside *There's Money Where Your Mouth Is: A Complete Insider's Guide to Earning Income and Building a Career in Voice-Overs* and *Voice-Overs for Podcasting.*

No book is print-worthy without a great editor. I thank Sarah Janssen at Skyhorse Publishing for her attention to detail. Turns out that words really ARE important!

Met hart en ziel, I thank my graphic designer genius Troy Ziel for deciphering my vague requests and delivering clean, clear, crisp graphics and logos for this book and many of my other business applications. Together, ZielCreative.com created my ElaineClarkVO.com website that won a SOVAS Outstanding Voiceover Website award!

I want to thank my clients and contributors who shared a variety of information and insights: Jordan Harbinger, creator, *The Jordan Harbinger Show*; Gabriel Mizrahi, producer and co-host, *The Jordan Harbinger Show*; Dan Avarkian, a.k.a., Dan the Produce Man, podcast host, *Fresh from the Field*; Dennis Strenk, host, *The People of Pathology Podcast*; Berlin Fisher, TV host for NBC Bay Area, *California Live;* Mylene Yao, M.D., co-founder and CEO, Univfy® Inc.; Peter Borruso, deputy public defender and trial attorney at law; Philip Wilder, teacher and mock trial coach; Martin L. Camp, professor of practice, SMU Dedman School of Law; Denis Eucalyptus, retired minister; Parker Eng, chairman of the board, Probe Ministries; Amelia Schimmel, PA announcer for the Athletics, Barracudas, Bay FC, and other sports; Anne Ganguzza, fashion and studio gear influencer; Wilson Walker, reporter, CBS News Bay Area; Joseph Schmitz, co-founder of Special Focus and owner, Eureka-Street Learning.

For the article in the Epilogue from *The Hindu Business Line* and being titled a "Communication Guru" in multiple newspapers in India, I thank

Balasubramanian Krishnan. He was CEO of NuVeda Learning when he brought me over to Chennai to write, perform, and share my communication techniques in a series of training modules and lead a seminar in Bangalore to a room full of India's top C-Suite executives.

To the companies that hired me to make a presentation, direct a tradeshow, or coach their employees and C-, V-, and D-level management, I thank you for the trust you put in me and the knowledge I gained from each of these experiences.

Insightful thanks to the news directors in the San Francisco and Sacramento areas who hired me to add a little polish and panache to some of their multimedia journalists, weather and traffic reporters, and anchors.

While I'd like to list every one of you, I thank all the students who worked with me, colleagues who supported me, podcasters who had me on their show, business associates who hired me in the U.S. and abroad, friends, relatives, and people who like to talk.

What a unique opportunity I've been given to lead people in all walks of life, improve their speech, and become better communicators. I wish you all the best!

Now it's time to re-read the book and tell your friends and colleagues to pick up their own copy because I want your book to be marked up, dog-eared, and dotted with Post-it notes.

Glossary

AUDIO DESCRIPTION: Voice actor performance in a film or TV show intended for blind audiences to have an immersive entertainment experience.

BACKSTORY: Life experiences, background, beliefs, and events that are often not stated but influence the behavior, motivation, and choices of the speaker's message.

BILLBOARD IT: Slowing down and adding emphasis to the client's name, title, main concept, or key phrases so those words stand out.

BODY POP: Quick initial movement used by a speaker on the first word or two to stop thinking and trust themself.

COLOR: Subtle nuances of speech that enhance keywords and phrases so they sound interesting, meaningful, and more memorable.

CTA, or Call to Action: An instruction intended to stimulate an audience's response.

EMOTION: Natural expression of how someone feels about a current or past moment.

ETHOS: Authority established to help the audience understand why they should trust the speaker.

FEEL AND TAKE ACTION: Delivering a message in a manner that elicits an emotional response from the audience and inspires them to take a specific action.

INTENTION: Tactics and actions used to lead the audience to the desired end result.

KINESTHETIC MOVEMENT: Physical movements, gestures, and actions that involve the body's sense of motion and spatial awareness in relation to surroundings and other objects to enhance learning and skill development.

LOGOS: Logic, facts, and evidence used to support a claim and appeal to the audience's reasoning.

MOTIVATION: Prior situation or "moment before" that connects the speaker to the opening words, so the message is personally and reactively fueled.

NEED: Defining one-word objective that clarifies the primary purpose and meaning of the entire message.

PATHOS: Appeal to the audience's emotions so they feel a desired way.
PERSONALIZE: Physically, mentally, emotionally, or imaginatively connecting with all or parts of the message by accessing past or present personal experiences.
POV, or Point of View: The perspective on the message that establishes the speaker's authority and opinion.
RESOLVE: Concluding statements that restate information and suggests a specific CTA: support, believe, trust, avoid, visit, purchase, join, subscribe, act now, engage, create, etc.
RESONANCE: Reverberations and vibrations that occur when sound passes through the mouth and sinus cavity and the timbre and intensity of the voice is enhanced.
RHETORIC: Art of persuasive and expressive language and writing.
RHETORICAL TRIANGLE: Three main appeals used to persuade an audience—ethos, logos, and pathos.
RHYTHM: The "music of speech" created melodic timing, pitch, word stress, quantity of syllables, and pauses.
SIBILANCE: A harsh or elongated "s" sound that can be reduced by minimizing the amount of contact with the tongue and roof of mouth and/or relaxing and lowering the jaw slightly.
STAIRSTEPPING: Musically separating words, phrases, and lists by progressively changing the pitch of each new item up, down, or zigzagged.
STORY ARC: Structuring a message so it takes the listener on a journey from introduction of problem, to content solutions, to resolution.
SUBSTITUTION: A performance approach used to mentally relate to a person, place, thing, or real-life event that generates the desired emotional and physical response.
SUBTEXT: The underlying thoughts, feelings, motivations, needs, and intentions that are not explicitly stated but are communicated through actions, expressions, body language, tone of voice, and pauses.
TEMPO: Speed of speech based on the number of units or syllables spoken within a given amount of time.
THROW IT AWAY: Playing down information by speeding up on unimportant words or phrases. It is often accompanied by a flick of the hand or dismissive arm movement.
WARM IT UP: Smile and lighten up how the message is spoken.

INDEX

A

acknowledge step, in structure, 14–16
action
  backstory and, 27
  goals and, 30
  inspiring, 6, 28, 30–33
advocacy, 7
aggressive pointing, 80–81
airflow, 207
ambush journalism, 166
anxiety, 35
Aristotle, 3, 41
arms, 201
  in business setting, 110–111
  crossed, 81, 110, 201
  dead, 110
  at waist level, 111
attire, 20
attitude, 66–67
Atwood, Margaret, 6
audience
  casual, 4
  challenging, 31
  connection, 22
  distraction, 14, 17
  emotional reaction of, 13
  engagement, 28, 105–107, 124, 128
  familiar, 4
  formal, 4
  greeting, 15
  leading, 121
  needs of, 36–38
  nonreactive, 78
  not paying attention, 78
  questions, 13
  relationship, 3
  remembering, 138
  remote, 4
  role, 15
  thanking, 16
  truths of, 36–38
  unforeseen change in, 13
audiobooks, 163, 189
authenticity, 27, 108
authority, 64–65, 205, 209–210
Avakian, Dan, 116–117
awareness, 6

B

backstory, 26–27
barriers, breaking down, 25
belief, 184–185
Bernbach, Bill, 103
body language, 16–17, 19, 50, 64, 184, 187, 195, 201–203
  casual, 4
  formal, 4
body-voice coordination, 58–59
Borruso, Peter, 141
bridge, 34–38
business pitches, 124–125
business reporting, 152
business setting, 110–112

C

call and response, 20
call to action (CTA), 32
Camp, Martin L., 145
celebration, 7
ceremonial style, 188
change leadership, 6
charisma, 209
checklists, 84
clarity, 5
coercive authority, 209
comedic style, 188
compassionate style, 188
conference room, 122–123
confidence, 36, 64, 100–101
conflict resolution, 7
connection, 5, 6
"cons," 165–166
context, 26, 28
continuity, 28
conversational style, 18–19, 108, 188
co-speaker drop out, 14
costume, 20
counseling, religious, 148
creativity, 6
credibility, 6, 27, 28
cross-platform interviews, 108

D

deadlines, micro-, 84
debate style, 18, 188
decisions, 6
delegated authority, 210
delivery
  casual, 4
  formal, 4
  intentions and, 49–50
  message and, 5
demonstrations, 11, 20
demonstrative style, 188
diaphragm, 206–207
didactic style, 18
disabilities, 167–177
disorganization, 89–90
documentary, 163–164
Durant, William, 39

E

economic reporting, 152
Eisenhower Matrix, 89–90
Emerson, Ralph Waldo, 1
emotional arc, 216
emotional colors, 194–195
emotional connection, 26
emotional contrast, 194
emotional intensity, 194
emotional landscape, 195
emotional problem, 215
emotional resonance, 26
emotions, 53–54, 55, 63, 205, 211
empowerment, 6
ending, strong, 121–122
energy levels, 16
Eng, Parker, 148–149
engagement, 105–107, 124, 128
  of audience, 28
  casual, 4
  enhancing, 25
  formal, 4
  in how, 11
engage step, in structure, 19–21
entertaining style, 187
entertainment, 7
entertainment reporting, 152
ethos, 39–40, 205
Eucalyptus, Denis, 146–148
evocative style, 188
examples, 10
exiting stage, 122
expert authority, 209
extemporaneous style, 18, 187
eye contact, 15
eyes, 203

F

facial expressions, 195
fast talking, 97
fear, of public speaking, 93–94
feedback, 5, 16
feet, 202
fidgeting, 79–80, 110
field reporting, 152
Fisher, Berlin, 135–136
focus
  inward, 91
  visual, 121
forgetting, 78
formal style, 18, 187

G

gaming, 165–166
Ganguzza, Anne, 161
gestures, 9, 68–70, 79–82, 92, 187, 197, 204
graphics, 109
growth, 7
guesting, 135–138
guidance, 7

H

hand(s), 9
  in business setting, 110–111
  cupped, 111
  movements, 68–70, 79–82, 187, 197
  in pockets, 81–82, 110, 111
  at waist level, 111
Harbinger, Jordan, 115
health reporting, 152
history, personal, 24–25
hosting, 135–138
how, 10–11
Hubbard, Elbert, 77
humanization, 27
humor, 17, 183
hydration, 206

I

imagination, 181–182
I'm a Tree, 174–175
impromptu style, 18, 187
improvisation, 20
influence, 6
influencers, 160–161
informal authority, 209
informal style, 18, 187
informative style, 187
inspiration, 6
inspirational style, 18
intentions, 49–50, 55, 58–60, 211
interaction, 17
interpretative spin, 183–184
interviews, 108–109, 132–134
investigative reporting, 152

J

job interviews, 132–134
Jobs, Steve, 180
journalism, ambush, 166
journalist, multimedia, 154–155

L

language
  casual, 4
  formal, 4
  inclusive, 15
  simple, 11
large stage, 120–122
legacy, 7
legal settings, 141–145

life experience, 182
Lincoln, Abraham, 79
listening, 5
logic, 205
logos, 40, 205
Look What I Found, 175–176

M

Magic Box, 173–174
Making It M.I.N.E.®
 emotions in, 53–54, 55, 63, 211
 intentions in, 49–50, 55, 58–60, 211
 motivation in, 47–49, 55, 56–57, 61, 211
 need in, 51–53, 55, 60–63, 211
 overview of, 47–54
May I Sit in Your Chair?, 170–171
meaning, 26
media prep, 137
Mehrabian, Albert, 215
memorability, 26
midline, 70
mindfulness, 36
ministry, 147–148
Mirror, 172
mistakes, 78, 138
Mizrahi, Gabriel, 115–116
mock trial, 142–144
Molière, 73
mood, 17
moral authority, 209
motivation, 47–49, 55, 56–57, 61, 211
movement adjustments, 79–82
multimedia journalist, 154–155

N

narrative-driven interviews, 108
narrative style, 188
need, 51–53, 55, 60–63, 211
needs, 34–35, 37
Newman, Ernest, 86
news, 150–156
news anchor, 150–151
Newton, Isaac, 5
noun intentions, 58

O

"Once Upon a Time . . ." Story, 176–177
opening moment, 120
opinion, 66–67
oratorical style, 188
over-analysis, 91
overthinking, 36, 91–92
overwhelm, 91

P

pacing, 17, 194
panels, 153–154, 165–166
pathos, 41–42, 205
pauses, dramatic, 19
personal communication style, 113
personal history, 24–25
personalization, 181–185
persuasive authority, 210
persuasive style, 18, 187
physical interaction, 20–21
Picasso, Pablo, 30
pitches, 124–125
pitfalls, performance, 75–76
podcasting, 114–118, 189
pointing, 9, 80–81, 110
pointless movements, 82
political reporting, 152
politics, 130–131
positional authority, 209
posture, 201
power box, 68–70
preparation, 91–92
presentations, 119–125
pride, 64–65
prior moment, 27–29
process identification, 10
procrastination, 83–85
progress tracking, 85
props, 20
purpose, 5

Q

questions
 audience, 13
 uncomfortable, 78

R

rapport, 25
react step, in structure, 16–17
reading the room, 15, 37
recap, 137
relatability, 25–26, 138
relationship
 audience, 3
religious settings, 146–149
repetition, 13, 138
reporter, 151–153
Rhetorical Triangle, 39, 117, 205, 220
rhythm, 20
Roosevelt, Eleanor, 34

S

sales, 139–145
Schimmel, Amelia, 157, 158–159
Schmitz, Joseph, 167
script techniques, 208
self-consciousness, 91
self-reflection, 31
self-shielding stance, 111
sermons, 147
setting change, 20
Shakespeare, William, 7
shoulders, 202
silence, 78
sincerity, 119
slow talking, 98–99, 119
small group presentation, 122–123
social media, 135–138, 160–161, 189
Sound Ball, 168–170
spatial indications, 9
speaking at, 105–106
speaking to, 106
speaking with, 106–107
speak step, in structure, 17–19
special needs, 167–177
speeches, 126–129
spinning, of bad to good, 77–78
sports, 157–159
sports reporting, 152
stage shapes, 69
status, 22–24
steepling fingers, 111
step-by-step explanations, 10
storytelling, 20, 71–72, 191–192
storytelling style, 18
strengths, 186
Strenk, Dennis, 117–118
structure
 acknowledge step in, 14–16
 casual, 4
 engage step in, 19–21
 formal, 4
 react step in, 16–17
 speak step in, 17–19
 think step in, 11–14
subtext, 72
surprise, 21
swaying, 80
Swindoll, Charles R., 10–11

T

tailoring, of message, 15
tapping, 9
task
 break down, 84
 prioritization, 84
technical glitches, 78
technology reporting, 152
TED Talks, 128–129, 189
television, 135–138
tells, 196–199
think step, in structure, 11–14
throat clearing, 206
time blocks, 84–85
time cut, last-minute, 13
tone, 194
 casual, 4
 formal, 4
 intentions and, 49–50
topic change, by host, 13
tradeshows, 123–124
traffic reporting, 152
train of thought, 78
transparency, 77
trust, 36
trust building, 25
truth, projection of, 197–199
truths, 35–36, 37–38
Tyson, Margaret, 21

U

understanding, 6
uptalk, 95–96
urgency, 31

V

values, common, 24–25
venue change, 14
verb intentions, 58
virtual interviews, 132–133
visuals, 11, 109, 121, 122–123
vocal variety, 19
voice
 fatigue, 123–124
 pitch of, 86–88, 196
 resting, 206
 strain, 123–124
voice-overs, 162–164
volume, 194
vulnerability, 24, 36

W

Walker, Wilson, 155–156
warm-up, 207
water, 206
weaknesses, 186
weather reporting, 152
Welty, Eudora, 8
what, 5
when, 7–8
where, 8–10
who, 3–5
why, 6–7
Wilder, Philip, 144
wins, easy, 85
Wooden, John, 75
word emphasis, 59–60

Y

Yao, Mylene, 140
YouTube, 189

About the Author

Elaine A. Clark started her professional performance career as a stage actor. Soon after, she began a voice-over career and performing in on-camera business videos, corporate tradeshows, and film roles. The transition from four-to-six-week-long stage rehearsals to "snap your finger perform now" immediacy was startling! Often, the tried-and-true methods of rehearsal and practice took too long. There had to be a quicker way! So, she started developing her own technique to be "in the moment" and "connect with the audience" quickly and effectively.

Elaine started what many consider to be the first Voice-Over & Acting School in 1986, which she sold thirty-two years later. From those beginnings, she perfected her system for breaking through to the truth of the message, dropping it deeper in the body, reacting to the "moment before," and creating a story arc that connects with the one-word "need" of the speaker and listener.

Also, as a director and performer in video games, talking toys, business narrations, e-learning, anime, animation, commercials, and film, Elaine saw the value of how the breath holds emotions, muscle tension in specific parts of the body shape and form a character, and movements trigger muscle memory emotional recall.

For ten years, Elaine Clark and her business partner Joseph Schmitz were awarded grants to create an improvisation program in Northern California schools and camps targeted to special needs students. The kinesthetic movement and imaginative improv techniques opened up a whole new way of teaching through actions and reactions. For a copy of the instruction manual, go to ElaineClarkVO.com/special-focus to download the Special Focus workbook.

Elaine Clark has traveled the globe working with large and small companies to improve the communication skills of individuals and groups in an assortment of business and performance settings. She's the author of *There's Money Where Your Mouth Is* and *Voice-Overs for Podcasting.* Her voice and diction apps, *Activate Your Voice* and *Adding Melody to Your Voice*, provide quick voice warm-ups and speech musicality training. As a podcaster, Elaine Clark's *Real Talking Tips* offers speech communication tips, training, insights, and information. Her ElaineClarkVO.com newsletters present a deep dive into numerous and varied communication topics. And for theatergoers, check out the interactive play she co-wrote with Scott Munson, *R-III*-Actor You're Killing Me . . . a farce*, a hilarious tale of the perils of bad acting.

In addition to hosting her own podcast, Elaine A. Clark is a guest speaker on numerous podcasts and a guest speaker and presenter at conferences and events. To find out more or to schedule a coaching session for you or your group, visit her website: ElaineClarkVO.com.